To Be Like Jesus

DEVELOPING A CHRISTIAN LIFE-STYLE

Rob Burkhart

GOSPEL PUBLISHING HOUSE

SPRINGFIELD, MISSOURI

02–0658

Library of Congress Catalog Card Number 89-82758
International Standard Book Number 0–88243–658–9
Printed in the United States of America

Contents

Foreword

To be like Jesus,
To be like Jesus,
All I ask,
To be like Him;
All thru life's journey,
From earth to glory,
All I ask,
To be like Him.[1]

I don't remember when I learned that little chorus. But I do remember singing it again and again at church and wondering if anyone, especially me, could be like Jesus. He is the divine son of God, sinless and perfect. I am a natural son of Adam, painfully aware of my sin and imperfections. "To be like Jesus" seemed impossible.

Years later, after Bible college and seminary, I was asked to preach in a little church in my hometown. As I stood at the pulpit, I noticed a small sign, a message to the preacher from the congregation. It said simply:

"Sir, we would see Jesus."

I was struck by the reality of what those people longed for in their preacher. They were not interested in an educated and eloquent sermon. They longed for someone whose words and life embodied the Living Word.

I couldn't help but wonder if they would see Jesus in me that morning. *Did I, as Christ's messenger, reflect His person and presence? Was I like Jesus?*

The church of Jesus Christ has been called to the greatest task in all of human history: bringing the life of Christ to a dying world. For nearly 2,000 years its members have faithfully worked and sacrificed to fulfill the Church's mission. Yet today millions still have never heard the gospel. Millions more who live in "Christian" lands have rejected the claims of Christ in favor of Eastern religions, cults, or the pleasure-seeking and materialism of Western society. How can that be?

Although Jesus' earthly ministry lasted only 3 years, He drew thousands of followers to himself. One hundred and twenty of His disciples, filled with the Holy Spirit, spread the gospel around the world. Those men and women were poor, persecuted, and politically powerless. They lacked the great technology and wealth the church possesses today. Yet they accomplished what we have failed to do. They reached their world.

Could it be that their success is accounted for in the words of that old gospel chorus? They were like Jesus and, because they were, lost men and women were drawn to their message and to the living Christ. That simple process literally revolutionized all of human history and the eternal destinies of uncounted millions of people.

With all our technology, wealth, and training have we forgotten the key element of a Christian witness: a truly Christian life-style?

Kipling's short story "Lispeth" tells of an orphan from a mountain tribe who was reared by Christian missionaries in colonial India. The child grew up in their home and became a Christian. As a young woman Lispeth fell in love with an Englishman. Her love was spurned because of her race, and she was deceived by her adoptive parents. Thus confronted with racism and dishonesty, she left the mission station and returned to her people and their paganism.

Kipling's vivid account illustrates the problem. Lispeth was won by the claims of Christ and lost by the lives of His followers.

She preferred honest paganism to hypocritical Christianity. So do many today.

The purpose of this book is to examine the mission of Christian education and its method. To understand the mission we must define a Christian life-style, understand why Christians don't always live up to what they believe, and discover the steps to developing a truly Christian life-style. In examining the method, we must look at both the process and the principles of life-style education and apply those principles to the Sunday school.

I want to thank several important people for the opportunity to share this vision of Sunday school. First, I want to thank my Sunday school teachers. They invested their lives in mine when there seemed to be little or no possibility of a return on that investment. I hope they feel they invested well.

I want to thank my wife, Linda, and my children for their loving support. It's trite but true, nothing of any value is accomplished alone. I couldn't have done it without them.

I also want to thank my parents, who made their faith in Christ a life-style. Growing up in their home I saw firsthand what it meant to be a Christian every day. They have been and are my constant inspiration.

In addition, I want to thank the people in the Assemblies of God Sunday School Department. They believed in me and gave me the chance to write. It is not enough to believe you have something of value to say. You also need the opportunity to say it. I pray their trust is well rewarded.

Finally, I want to thank God. He knows why.

NOTES

[1]*Melody Choruses* (Springfield, Mo.: Gospel Publishing House, 1963), 3.

1

The Christian Life-Style: The Goal

I had a bad case of culture shock!

We had come to Santa Cruz, Bolivia, to help the people of Maranatha Assembly build a new church. I was not prepared for what I saw. Bolivia is like many other parts of the Third World. A few Bolivians have great wealth, but most live in grinding poverty. It got to me, especially the children and the beggars.

I was to preach in the morning service. We walked down a narrow dirt path past the construction site to a crude lean-to that had been serving the church as a sanctuary. The floors were dirt, the pews were rough benches, and the pulpit was a simple stand. Chickens scratched under the benches, and a stray dog wandered through. The differences between our beautiful new air-conditioned sanctuary in the United States and that church were jarring.

The pastor greeted us with a smile and a hug. He told us the people were in their Sunday school classes and the morning worship service would soon begin. So I looked for a place to pray. Preaching with an interpreter made me nervous, and I was gripped with a cold terror that I had nothing to say to the people.

There were some unfinished rooms in the church under construction where I could pray. As I walked into the half-finished building I heard a gentle voice. I peeked into the room and saw her. A Bolivian Sunday school teacher sat on a low stool with a ragged quarterly open in her lap. Gathered around her knees were 8 or 10 children intently listening as she told the Bible story. I do not speak Spanish, but suddenly I felt very much at home.

It is an almost universal scene. All around the world people gather to study and teach the Bible. Millions of dollars and millions of man hours are invested every year in Bible study. Many of us remember that special Sunday school teacher who invested his or her life and changed ours by teaching the Bible.

It is important that we understand why we teach the Bible. A clear vision of our mission will help determine our methods and measure our achievements.

Visions of the Sunday School

People have different visions of the Sunday school.

SUNDAY SCHOOL AND INFORMATION

We sat across from each other in a restaurant. He was a mature minister with years of experience. I was just out of seminary and beginning my ministry as a director of Christian education. I asked him what he believed was the Sunday school's purpose. He replied that he wanted the people in his church to know what the Bible taught and what the church believed.

For many, like my friend, the purpose of Sunday school is to communicate information about the Bible and the Christian faith. This vision has three aspects. First, the Sunday school ought to teach the Bible, all the Bible, and nothing but the Bible. The lives of Bible characters, Bible history, the structure and content of the books of the Bible, as well as an understanding of the biblical "big picture" are all important areas of study.

Next, this vision is concerned with how the church understands the Bible and communicates its teachings. There is a commitment to share the church's doctrinal position, history, and distinctives. Describing the differences between what "we" believe and what "they" believe is central in this vision. The

Sunday school becomes the primary way to communicate the unique identity of the church or the denomination.

The third aspect of this vision is the application of scriptural principles to the believer's life. The Bible is the guide for a person's life and faith. Understanding the rights, privileges, and responsibilities of the Christian life are the critical issues. The Sunday school's mission is to provide information relevant to believers' lives.

It is hard to argue with those goals. All Christians need to understand the Bible, God's revelation to man. All Christians need to understand their unique heritage and what their tradition has contributed. All Christians need to understand that what God says in the Bible is relevant to their lives.

That vision of Sunday school has become the dominant perspective for a number of reasons. First, virtually all those involved in Sunday school have been exposed to that vision through the public schools. The communication of information is the primary purpose of public education. Because public education is the most familiar model, the emphasis in Sunday school becomes *school.*

Second, in an information-based educational system, objectives can be clearly stated and tested. The student either has or has not mastered the information.

Finally, the information-based Sunday school is dominant because it is assumed that if people know the truth they will act in accordance with that truth. Those who do not must not know the truth or fully understand it. The solution is to provide more and better information.

One can see how widespread that assumption is in the way our society responds to many of its ills. For example, years ago the surgeon general determined that cigarette smoking is unhealthy. The government responded by placing warning labels on cigarette packages. The assumption was that if people understand smoking is a health hazard they will not smoke.

But the information-based vision of the Sunday school is not the only vision.

SUNDAY SCHOOL AND EMOTIONS

For others, the purpose of Christian education has as much to do with what the student feels as with what he knows. The experience is viewed in terms of its emotional (affective) impact, and proponents point out the importance of people's response to what they know.

Generally speaking, people respond to information by accepting it, rejecting it, or ignoring it. No matter which vision of Christian education the teacher holds, he or she wants the student to accept and value what is being taught and to develop a positive attitude toward God and the church. The student who understands what the Bible teaches, but rejects or ignores it breaks his Sunday school teacher's heart.

Christians need to develop biblically correct attitudes and values. It is not enough to understand that the Bible teaches believers to love their neighbors as themselves. The believer must come to love his neighbor. Christians are to actually feel content, not just to understand that godliness with contentment is great gain.

In this vision, the emphasis is on the student's experiencing God's power and presence. Supporters say Christian education must not only inform students about God, but must also create opportunities for the student to encounter God.

While recognizing the value of this vision, it must be noted that it is difficult to put into practice. First, we rarely have educational experiences in which our feelings are considered important educational outcomes. In public school, the teacher may want the students to like the subject, but ultimately it doesn't matter how they feel. Their grades will be determined by what they know, not by how they feel about the subject. It is easy to bring that same approach into the Sunday school.

Second, this vision is difficult to put into practice because it is hard to determine feeling goals and nearly impossible to determine if they have been achieved. To illustrate, it is easy to determine if a student has memorized John 3:16. It is much more difficult to know if he feels God's love and the joy of salvation.

Finally, this vision isn't put into practice because our society tends to value knowledge more than emotion. We are even suspicious of emotion in the church. Once a non-Pentecostal friend remarked that he and the people in his church worried about us Pentecostals. He was concerned that we would be "swept into error and excess by our emotionalism." Paramount in his vision of the Christian life were an understanding of and a commitment to solid doctrine, not attitude and emotion.

A suspicion of emotionalism has developed among some Pentecostals because of the excesses of a few. Like my friend, they fear people will be swept away from sound doctrine. The greater danger, however, is a passionless, empty religion that has "a form of godliness" but denies the power (2 Timothy 3:5).

SUNDAY SCHOOL AND BEHAVIOR

The Sunday school's task is more than communicating knowledge and shaping attitudes and values. Some see the purpose of Christian education in terms of what the student does. Advocates of this vision are concerned with holy living and preparing people for ministry. They believe understanding the Bible and developing proper attitudes are of little value if the student doesn't act on that knowledge and those attitudes.

Granted, holy living is more than observing a list of don'ts. But every believer must recognize that people who are fully committed to the cause of Christ do not do certain things. At its core, holiness means to be set aside for God's use. So not only are there things Christians *do not do,* there are also things true Christians *must do.* Teaching believers to act like Christians is a key aspect of this vision.

A second aspect of this vision of the Sunday school focuses on the need to equip people for involvement in ministry inside and outside the church. Training Christians to be effective witnesses, courteous ushers, proficient Sunday school teachers, godly parents, and a host of other important ministries is seen as a vital function of the Sunday school.

Educators have long emphasized the importance of action and warned against its absence.

> [Moral education] is not an inculcation of moral precepts or a teaching of moral attitudes. This Sunday-school approach produces Sunday-school results: [people] who mouth the appropriate platitudes on demand but who go about their weekday affairs without a moment's concern for the implications of their actions. Moral education involves simply showing people what they are really doing. And it is aimed, not at those who lack practical wisdom or moral virtue, but at those who, possessing these characteristics, nevertheless fail to do as they ought because "they do not know what they do."[1]

This vision of Christian education is publicly applauded and privately avoided. Teachers may be reluctant to focus on conduct for a number of reasons. First, like every other Christian, Sunday school teachers are painfully aware of their own failures and feel uncomfortable challenging their students to act in ways they themselves have not acted.

It is also avoided because we remember the excesses of our legalistic past. Those of us who grew up in the holiness/Pentecostal movement are sometimes embarrassed by "clothesline" preaching and teaching. It is a sad irony that as our society has grown more and more sinful the church has become less and less willing to speak out against sin. As we have become more concerned with fitting into society than with changing it, the church has adopted a tolerant, anything-goes attitude. It is far easier to focus on knowledge and hope that it will somehow work its way into behavior.

Evaluating the Visions

The three visions of the Sunday school that we have discussed are like the legs of a three-legged stool. Each of them is necessary but is insufficient by itself. Take any one of them away and the Sunday school's effectiveness is severely damaged. Combine them and a strong, effective educational ministry will emerge. Balancing all three concerns is difficult, but it is the biblical model of Christian education. In Deuteronomy 31:11,12, God commanded Moses,

> Read this law before them in their hearing. Assemble the people—men, women and children, and the aliens living in your towns—so they can listen and learn to fear the Lord your God and follow carefully all the words of this law.

First, the people were to "listen and learn." They were to pay attention and understand "the words of this law." They were to learn to fear and reverence the Lord. Finally, they were to "follow carefully" or to act in accordance with the law they had heard.

Our students should do the same.

The Purpose of Sunday School

If the biblical model of Christian education incorporates knowledge, emotion, and action, what is its purpose? We find it in Christ's own words when He gave the Church its marching orders in Matthew 28:18–20:

> Then Jesus came to them and said, "Go and make disciples of all nations, baptizing them in the name of the Father and of the Son and of the Holy Spirit, and teaching them to obey everything I have commanded you. And surely I will be with you always, to the very end of the age."

The Great Commission focuses our attention on the basic elements of our teaching ministry. First, we are to teach everything Christ commanded. The church is the caretaker of God's revelation to man. As each generation passes that revelation on to the next, the truth of the gospel spreads throughout the world and across time.

Second, the church is to teach obedience to Christ. It is not enough to understand the gospel. One must live it. Obedience is both an attitude and an action. We are not called to the grudging obedience of a slave but the willing submission of a son. God is not looking for religious ritual but hearts that love to obey (Isaiah 1:10–20). "This is love for God: to obey his commands" (1 John 5:3).

Finally, teaching is a process that begins and ends with relationships. Paul emphasized this when he told Timothy, "The things you have heard me say in the presence of many witnesses entrust to reliable men who will also be qualified to teach others" (2 Timothy 2:2). The quality of the teacher's relationship with his or her students and the students' relationships with one another are powerful parts of the teaching process.

We are called to be like Jesus and to teach others how to be like Him. The goal of Christian education is nothing less than developing an authentic Christian life-style.

Life-Style Defined

Simply put, a *life-style* is an individual's "whole way of living."[2] Another definition of life-style focuses on the "tendencies toward certain kinds of behaviors that are persistent and distinctive and make [the person] a unique personality."[3]

A life-style has four aspects: unity, consistency, actuality, and development.

UNITY

Unity is the "whole way of living." A person's life-style integrates the way he thinks, feels, acts, and interacts.

The kind of life-style a person develops depends on many factors. Interests, income, age, relationships, background, and work are all significant. It is the unique uniting of those factors that produces a life-style.

One facet of a person's life may become so important that it determines his entire life-style. For instance, a person training for Olympic competition will develop a life-style very different from that of his peers. Everything in the athlete's life is focused on a single goal: to win the Olympic gold medal.

Paul used the athlete's training life-style as an analogy of the Christian life-style:

> Do you not know that in a race all the runners run, but only one gets the prize? Run in such a way as to get the prize. Everyone who competes in the games goes into strict training. They do it to get a crown that will not last; but we do it to get a crown that will last forever. Therefore I do not run like a man running aimlessly; I do not fight like a man beating the air. No, I beat my body and make it my slave so that after I have preached to others, I myself will not be disqualified for the prize (1 Corinthians 9:24–27).

Like the athlete, Christians must unite all their energies and all facets of their lives to win their race; to "press on toward the goal to win the prize for which God has called [us] . . . in Christ Jesus" (Philippians 3:14).

Unity, as a quality of the Christian life-style, was clearly in Christ's mind when He responded to the question, "Which is the greatest commandment in the Law?" He replied,

> " 'Love the Lord your God with all your heart and with all your soul and with all your mind.' This is the first and greatest commandment. And the second is like it: 'Love your neighbor as yourself' " (Matthew 22:37–39).

A believer's life-style unites intellect, emotions, actions, and relationships.

CONSISTENCY

A life-style is a complex pattern of behaviors that are consistently acted on over a long period of time. The fact that a person does something occasionally does not make it part of his life-style. Occasionally attending church doesn't make one a Christian anymore than periodically playing basketball makes one an athlete.

Paul encouraged his Corinthian readers to consistency. "Stand firm," he urged. "Let nothing move you. Always give yourselves fully to the work of the Lord, because you know that your labor in the Lord is not in vain" (1 Corinthians 15:58).

ACTUALITY

A person's life-style is what he actually does; how he really lives. It is not how he wishes he had lived or believes he should live. The individual creates a life-style from each decision he makes, from the possibilities he chooses to make real. It is a basic biblical principle:

> A man reaps what he sows. The one who sows to please his sinful nature, from that nature will reap destruction; the one who sows to please the Spirit, from the Spirit will reap eternal life (Galatians 6:7,8).

It may be argued that a person cannot choose everything that goes into making up his life-style. One does not choose his sex, race, family, when or where he is born, or what personality and abilities he inherits. All of those are powerful factors in shaping a life-style; however, there still are real choices to be made.

Let me illustrate. The ladies in my home church make beautiful quilts to raise money for missions. Most of the fabric is donated so they do not have a lot of choice in the material with which they work. But they have *total control* over what they *do* with the fabric they have.

Building a life-style is something like sewing a quilt. We cannot choose what life hands us, but we can choose what we do with our lives.

DEVELOPMENT

Development is the final quality of a life-style. A person's life-style should grow, change, and evolve within the continuity of life. On the surface, that may seem to contradict the quality of consistency. But it doesn't. Consistency addresses the broad themes of a person's life that are carried out over long periods of time. Development speaks of the changes that occur within those broad themes.

Marriage may last most or all of one's adult life. But within that life-style is true development. The life-style of a newlywed couple with no children will change and develop when a child is born. Raising small children is different from raising teenagers. Other changes occur as the children grow older and leave home. Finally, the life-style of a retired, elderly couple is yet another stage in the development of the married life-style. Being married is a consistent life-style that contains many stages of development.

Paul talks about that kind of development in the Christian life-style. He directs the Ephesian believers to "no longer be infants, tossed back and forth by the waves, and blown here and there" but to "grow up into him who is the Head, that is, Christ" (Ephesians 4:14,15).

Both "infant" and "grown-up" believers are living a Christian life-style, but they are in different stages of development. Just as a healthy child develops physically, the healthy Christian develops spiritually.

A Christian Life-Style Defined

Who has a Christian life-style? The person who has committed his whole life to Christ. All facets of life—work, family, personal habits, finances, attitudes, and affections—are united in the cause of serving Christ. The faith of a person living a Christian life-style is just as visible at work, at home, or at play as it is in church.

A Christian life-style is also marked by dependability. No matter what happens in life, a person who is committed to Christ evidences a steady, solid faith that can go the distance. Those who are unstable in their commitment lack an essential component of a truly Christian life-style.

Talk really is cheap. People may talk about the way Christians should live, but unless they actually live that way they cannot be said to have a Christian life-style. Living the Christian life really is easier said than done. But that is our calling. We are to obey everything Christ commanded. When we do so to the best of our ability, we can claim an authentic Christian life-style.

Finally, the Christian life-style is one of growth. The believer puts "childish ways" behind him (1 Corinthians 13:11) and grows "in the grace and knowledge of our Lord and Savior Jesus Christ" (2 Peter 3:18). Like a child who does not develop physically or mentally, the believer who does not mature in his faith is a tragedy. Without spiritual growth there can be no truly Christian life-style.

NOTES

[1] David P. Gauthier, "Moral Action and Moral Education" in *Moral Education: Interdisciplinary Approaches,* eds. C.M. Beck, B.S. Crittenden, and E.V. Sullivan (New York: Newman Press, 1971), 146.

[2] *Webster's New World Dictionary* (New York: Warner Books, 1984).

[3] Martha M. Leypoldt, *Learning Is Change: Adult Education in the Church* (Valley Forge, Pa.: Judson Press, 1971), 40.

2

Qualities of the Christian Life-Style

An amazing incident is recorded in Acts 4. Shortly after the Day of Pentecost, Peter and John were arrested for preaching Jesus and disturbing the peace. Actually, the beggar who had been crippled from birth created the disturbance when Peter and John healed him by the power and in the name of Jesus (Acts 3:7,8).

The apostles were arrested and hauled into court before "the rulers, elders and teachers of the law" (Acts 4:5). They demanded that Peter and John explain what had happened.

After Peter had responded, the Jewish leaders "saw the courage of Peter and John and realized that they were unschooled, ordinary men, [and] they were astonished and . . . took note that these men had been with Jesus" (Acts 4:13).

Amazing! Peter and John conducted themselves in such a way that their connection to Christ was undeniable. Even their enemies had to admit that what made them different was that they "had been with Jesus."

There ought to be an undeniable connection between the Christ we serve and the life we live. It should account for a life-style that is different from that of our unsaved neighbor. Tragically, and all too often, there is little or no difference.

We have said Christian living is the goal and method of all Christian education. Further, the expression *Christian living* means all of one's personality is integrated into and acts in accordance with behavior we call Christian. The thoughts, emotions, desires, and actions of a person flow together and form a behavior pattern or a life-style that is uniquely Christian.[1]

Understanding that, we recognize a study of the Christian life-style must deal with four critical areas: the mind, the heart, behavior, and relationships.[2]

The Mind

The intellect is the part of man that is capable of thinking, understanding, and knowing. But the mind is more than a place to deposit facts. It is the means by which we perceive the world around us—our worldview. Facts are objective, but the meaning of those facts varies with each person. For instance, the same half glass of water may be viewed as half full or as half empty. The issue is not how much water is in the glass. The issue is the perspective of the person who sees the glass.

The Bible describes two kinds of minds—natural and spiritual. These differing views of the world can and do come into conflict. The believer must choose whether to have the mind of Christ or the world's "mind."

Twentieth-century America has a "mind," a worldview, that shapes our perception of reality. Like any other belief system, the secular American worldview makes certain assumptions. It considers God irrelevant. Whether or not God exists does not really matter. It assumes the absolute supremacy of human reason. With science and the scientific method to guide, human progress is seen as inevitable. The self-sufficiency and centrality of man are assumed. Finally, evolution is viewed as absolute truth.

The Bible evaluates this "natural mind." First, it is closed to the claims of Christ because "the god of this age has blinded the minds of unbelievers, so that they cannot see the light of the gospel" (2 Corinthians 4:4).

Second, the natural mind is deceived. "Just as Eve was deceived by the serpent's cunning," so people can "be led astray from ... sincere and pure devotion to Christ" (2 Corinthians 11:3).

Third, the natural mind is reprobate. Those who "did not think it worthwhile to retain the knowledge of God" have been given "over to a depraved mind, to do what ought not to be done" (Romans 1:28). They "have been robbed of the truth" (1 Timothy 6:5) and "oppose the truth" (2 Timothy 3:8).

Finally, the natural mind is conceited. A person's "unspiritual mind puffs him up with idle notions" (Colossians 2:18).

The "spiritual mind," however, has been renewed and is "able to test and approve what God's will is—his good, pleasing and perfect will" (Romans 12:2). In writing about this new mind, Paul tells the believer:

> Put off your old self, which is being corrupted by deceitful desires; to be made new in the attitude of your minds; and to put on the new self, created to be like God in true righteousness and holiness (Ephesians 4:22–24).

The spiritual mind is in touch with the mind of God. "I will put my laws in their minds and write them on their hearts. I will be their God, and they will be my people" (Hebrews 8:10). It is "a slave to God's law" (Romans 7:25). Finally, it is the mind of Christ (Philippians 2:5–8). In this passage, Christ is described as sacrificing His deity, humbling himself, and becoming obedient to His work on the cross. In the same way, the believer who has the mind of Christ willingly sacrifices, humbles himself, and obeys God's voice.

The Heart

The second area in which a Christian life-style should be evident is our feelings. The Bible speaks of the heart as the center of physical, emotional, and spiritual life. It is the seat of the emotions, the will, desires, attitudes, and moral life. Feelings both motivate and control human behavior.

In the biblical view, the heart is seen as the prime mover of human behavior. Jesus said, "Out of the heart come evil thoughts, murder, adultery, sexual immorality, theft, false testimony, slander" (Matthew 15:19). The "good man brings good things out of the good stored up in his heart," but "the evil man brings evil things out of the evil stored up in his heart" (Luke 6:45). Behavior flows out of the beliefs, attitudes, and values of the heart.

The biblical concept of the heart also recognizes its controlling influence on feelings and desires. "All of us also lived among them [the disobedient] at one time, gratifying the cravings of our sinful nature and following its desires and thoughts" (Ephesians 2:3). Solomon spoke of following his heart's desires. "I denied myself nothing my eyes desired; I refused my heart no pleasure. My heart took delight in all my work" (Ecclesiastes 2:10).

People ought to control their feelings and not the other way around. Lack of control has disastrous but often unforeseen results:

> Each one [of us] is tempted when, by his own evil desire, he is dragged away and enticed. Then, after desire has conceived, it gives birth to sin; and sin, when it is full-grown, gives birth to death (James 1:14,15).

The believer's heart is to be pure. We are to seek first the kingdom of God (Matthew 6:33), love God with all our hearts (Mark 12:30), and "not love the world or anything in the world" (1 John 2:15). Finally, we are told, "Come near to God and he will come near to you. . . . purify your hearts" (James 4:8). If our affections are purified, we will desire God's will and ways.

The source of our hearts' desires ought to be God. "Delight yourself in the Lord and he will give you the desires of your heart" (Psalm 37:4). Many understand this verse to say that if a person delights himself in the Lord, God will give him whatever he wants. Some people think they can manipulate God and get what they want by being nice to Him. They are wrong.

The believer is promised not just the object of the desire but the desire itself. If a person "delights" in the Lord, he makes God the most important thing in his life. He comes to want the same things God wants. Certainly God blesses His children or delights in giving them good things. But the godly heart wants God more than anything else.

The godly heart is near to God. In Hebrews 10:22, believers are encouraged to "draw near to God with a sincere heart in full assurance of faith, having our hearts sprinkled to cleanse us from a guilty conscience."

It is in our hearts that we believe God raised Jesus from the dead (Romans 10:9,10). And in our hearts, we are to "set apart Christ as Lord" (1 Peter 3:15). Then the "peace of Christ" will rule in our hearts (Colossians 3:15).

A believer with a truly Christian life-style will also have a godly heart. His will, attitudes, desires, and emotions are captivated by his love for God. All aspects of his feelings are brought into submission to the lordship of Christ.

Behavior

Having a Christian life-style is not confined to believing the right things or having the right attitudes and feelings. Being a Christian is also about how one lives every day. Holy living is the call of God (2 Corinthians 6:17), the command of God (1 Peter 1:16), and a requirement for anyone who hopes to have a relationship with God (Hebrews 12:14).

But what constitutes holy living? God calls us to holy living in several specific areas of life. First, believers are to offer their "bodies as living sacrifices, holy and pleasing to God—which is . . . spiritual worship" (Romans 12:1). It matters how we use our bodies. We "are God's temple and . . . God's Spirit lives . . ." in us. "If anyone destroys God's temple, God will destroy him; for God's temple is sacred, and you are that temple" (1 Corinthians 3:16,17).

The second area in which holy living is called for is in our actions: "Whatever you do, whether in word or deed, do it all in the name of the Lord Jesus, giving thanks to God the Father through him" (Colossians 3:17). Paul also wrote that believers are to put into practice what they have learned, received, heard, or seen (Philippians 4:9). The gospel was meant to be lived out not just talked about.

Our thought life is a third area in which we are called to holy living. Desire precedes action (James 1:15). Behavior is conceived in the thoughts long before it is carried out. Christians are to focus their thoughts on "whatever is true, whatever is noble, whatever is right, whatever is pure, whatever is lovely, whatever is admirable—if anything is excellent or praiseworthy" (Philippians 4:8). Purity in thought is essential to the Christian life-style.

Relationships

The final dimension of human behavior is the area of relationships. The Bible has much to say about the kind and quality of the believer's relationships.

When Jesus was asked what is the greatest commandment, He replied,

> " 'Love the Lord your God with all your heart and with all your soul and with all your mind.' This is the first and greatest commandment. And the second is like it: 'Love your neighbor as yourself.' All the Law and the Prophets hang on these two commandments" (Matthew 22:37–40).

There is to be an unbreakable bond between the believer's love for God and his love for others.

> If anyone says, "I love God," yet hates his brother, he is a liar. For anyone who does not love his brother, whom he has seen, cannot love God, whom he has not seen. And he has given us this command: Whoever loves God must also love his brother (1 John 4:20,21).

Six distinct qualities mark true Christian love. First, it is *sacrificial.* "Greater love has no one than this, that one lay down his life for his friends" (John 15:13). Sacrificial love was demonstrated by God. "This is love: not that we loved God, but that he loved us and sent his Son as an atoning sacrifice for our sins" (1 John 4:10).

Second, Christian love is *giving* love.

> Jesus Christ laid down his life for us. And we ought to lay down our lives for our brothers. If anyone has material possessions and sees his brother in need but has no pity on him, how can the love of God be in him? (1 John 3:16,17).

Third, Christian love is *active,* not passive sentiment. "Dear children, let us not love with words or tongue but with actions and in truth" (1 John 3:18). James wrote, "Suppose a brother or sister is without clothes and daily food. If one of you says to him, 'Go, I wish you well; keep warm and well fed,' but does nothing about his physical needs, what good is it?" (James 2:15,16).

Fourth, love of God and others is to be the highest *priority* of the Christian life. "These three remain: faith, hope and love. But the greatest of these is love" (1 Corinthians 13:13).

Fifth, true Christian love is also demonstrated by our *obedience.* " 'If anyone loves me, he will obey my teaching' " (John 14:23,24).

Finally, Christian love is *pure.* "Do not love the world or anything in the world. If anyone loves the world, the love of the Father is not in him" (1 John 2:15). Jesus said, "No servant can serve two masters. Either he will hate the one and love the other, or he will be devoted to the one and despise the other" (Luke 16:13).

Love is the cornerstone of the Christian's relationships. It is both Christ's command and example. " 'A new command I give you: Love one another. As I have loved you, so you must love one another. All men will know that you are my disciples if you love one another' " (John 13:34,35). A believer's relationships should be permeated by love. Without it, a truly Christian life-style cannot exist.

Peter and John were different. Their worldview, attitude, actions, and relationships had been radically changed because they had been with Jesus. The Jewish leaders knew what to do with ordinary, ignorant Galilean fishermen who caused trouble. But they did not know what to do with those disciples of Jesus. In the years that followed, the Jewish leaders tried everything in their power to destroy the Church. Nothing worked. Those early Christians, touched by Christ's power and presence, were unstoppable.

People like that still are.

NOTES

[1]James Michael Lee, *The Shape of Religious Instruction* (Mishawaka, Ind.: Religious Education Press, 1971), 11.

[2]Leypoldt, *Learning Is Change*, 44.

3

The Significance of a Christian Life-Style

Once there was an old sage who had an eager young disciple. The young man followed his master everywhere hoping to learn his secrets. He watched, listened, and learned as the old man carried on deep discussions with the wisest men of the day. But the young disciple felt his master's greatest secret eluded him, for at the end of every encounter the old man would turn to his disciple and ask him to withdraw. When the young man was out of earshot the old man would end the dialogue.

Finally the young man could stand it no longer. He confronted the sage, "Master, what is it you say after you send me away?"

"I ask a question—the most important question," replied the sage.

Thrilled at the thought of learning his master's greatest secret, the young man asked, "Master, what is it you ask?"

The old man paused as if he was a little embarrassed and then said, "I ask, 'So what?' "

Determining significance may be the most important issue in the world. If something is unimportant or makes no difference, then it is hardly worth our time. But something that is truly significant demands our attention and our action.

So why is living a consistent Christian life-style so important? After all, no one is perfect. Everyone fails at one time or another to live up to his or her beliefs. It is "normal" for people to be inconsistent.[1] Most people are in favor of living a consistent life-style, but are quick to point out that we do not live in a consistent world. Many try to develop a Christian life-style, but do not succeed.

Believers should strive to develop a consistent Christian life-style for several important reasons.

The Stigma of Inconsistency[2]

While people may recognize that everyone, including themselves, is capable of failing to live up to his or her beliefs, they still view such failures very negatively.

REPUTATION

Failure to live a consistent Christian life destroys the believer's reputation. Inconsistent people are described as selfish, hypocritical, stupid, silly, weak, dishonest, bad examples, untrustworthy, and lacking in personal pride. Their inconsistency is seen as damaging relationships, injuring themselves, hurting others, and blocking personal and spiritual growth.

The believer's reputation has significance beyond himself. It reflects on other Christians, the church, and the cause of Christ. It is trite but true: The only Bible some people will ever read is the lives of the Christians they know. A believer who does not live a consistent Christian life destroys not only his own credibility but also the credibility of the gospel.

I was returning home from conducting a Christian education seminar when I noticed a pastor who had participated in the seminar. He was leafing through an adult magazine at an airport newsstand. I wondered what his church and the people of his community would have thought of the gospel if they had seen him that day.

Paul wrote to the Corinthians that they were his letter of recommendation "read by everybody" and they should live in a way that demonstrated they were "a letter from Christ" (2 Corinthians 3:2,3). Paul's credibility as an apostle and Christ's reputation were dependent on their behavior.

Paul reminded Timothy that a deacon is to "have a good

reputation with outsiders, so that he will not fall into disgrace and into the devil's trap" (1 Timothy 3:7). And Peter urged his readers to "live such good lives among the pagans that . . . they may see your good deeds and glorify God" (1 Peter 2:12).

SELF-CONCEPT

Failure to live a consistent Christian life also damages a person's self-concept and leads to feelings of weakness and failure. As such it becomes a self-fulfilling prophecy. A person who sees himself as weak is more likely to fail. That failure reinforces the sense of weakness. It is a downward spiral of defeat and discouragement.

RELATIONSHIPS WITH OTHERS

All relationships are built on trust and love. Consistency and the trust it generates between people fuel society. It is hard, if not impossible, to imagine what a human society would be like if there were no consistency between what people say and what they do. It is precisely this kind of failure that destroys trust.

RELATIONSHIP WITH GOD

God's love and mercy are not tied to our performance. Salvation is not something we earn or deserve. However, we need to remember that God is holy and will not stand for sin. It was Adam and Eve's failure to live up to God's commandments that resulted in the loss of Eden and their separation from God. If we would enjoy a rich and full relationship with God, we must keep His commandments.

Although good works are not the source of our salvation, we should live differently because we have been saved. God's love and grace do not give us a license to sin. "Shall we go on sinning so that grace may increase? By no means!" (Romans 6:1,2). They give us the opportunity to become like Jesus. We can make mistakes, we can fail, and, if we repent—if we "leave [our] life of sin" (John 8:11)—our relationship with God can be restored. But we should never take sin lightly.

> If they have escaped the corruption of the world by knowing our Lord and Savior Jesus Christ and are again entangled in it and overcome, they are worse off at the end than they were at the beginning. It would have been better for them not to have known the way of righteousness, than to have known it and then to turn their backs on the sacred commandment that was passed on to them (2 Peter 2:20,21).

How does God view our failure to live up to His commands? God sets a high standard for His children, but He also realizes that we are engaged in a growth process. We are to "become mature, attaining to the whole measure of the fullness of Christ" (Ephesians 4:13). God is patient and understanding with His children as they grow.

It is not by accident that we call God our Father and we are called His children. Like a good parent, God trains His children. Like good children, we are to obey and grow. Like any good parent, God takes into account the child's stage of development. He expects more from the mature Christian than from a newborn.

But no parent will tolerate rebellious disobedience and a stubborn unrepentant attitude. When a child rebelliously refuses to do what is right and refuses to ask for forgiveness, the relationship cannot be restored. In Christ's Parable of the Prodigal Son, the relationship between the father and younger son was restored only when the son left his rebellious life-style, returned to his father, and sought forgiveness (Luke 15:11–31).

The Value of Consistency

INFLUENCE

People should be consistent because of their influence on others. Very few of us realize the impact our lives have. We are being watched by our families, friends, acquaintances, and even people we do not know.

Several years ago my father was doing some shopping. A young mother from our church and her son were in the same store. Suddenly the little boy jumped up, pointed his finger at my father, and shouted at the top of his lungs, "Look, Mommy. There's Jesus!" Naturally, Dad—and everyone else in the store—was shocked at the child's insistence that he had seen Jesus.

It took some detective work, but later the child's mother was able to explain. It seems that in the boy's Sunday school class the children had been told that they were giving their offering to Jesus. My father, in his duties as the assistant superintendent, collected the Sunday school offerings from the classrooms. The little boy had drawn a logical conclusion. The children gave their money to Jesus, and Jesus came to get it!

That story illustrates how important it is to live a consistent Christian life. My father had no way of knowing the little boy had identified him as Jesus. It is frightening to think about the damage that could have been done if the boy had seen my father do something he should not. But all believers are in the same position. People are watching us and expecting Christlike behavior.

Paul lived in such a way that he was able to say, "Follow my example, as I follow the example of Christ" (1 Corinthians 11:1). We too should strive to be like Jesus for the sake of those who will follow us. We can lead others to Christ if we are following Him. But we can just as easily lead them away from Christ if our behavior is inconsistent with the gospel's teachings.

PERSONAL GROWTH

Developing a consistent Christian life-style is a way to grow in our Christian life. It is the goal we are to strive for. Paul understood the importance of this process in his life. He wrote to his Philippian readers:

> Not that I have already obtained all this, or have already been made perfect, but I press on to take hold of that for which Christ Jesus took hold of me. Brothers, I do not

consider myself yet to have taken hold of it. But one thing
I do: Forgetting what is behind and straining toward what
is ahead, I press on toward the goal to win the prize for
which God has called me heavenward in Christ Jesus.

All of us who are mature should take such a view of
things. . . . Only let us live up to what we have already
attained (Philippians 3:12–16).

That striving, that process of becoming like Jesus, is a valuable part of the Christian life. It is in the striving that we learn
important lessons and gain valuable insights into who we are,
the meaning of our own lives, and, most important, the nature
of our relationship with God. The believer who strives for a
consistent Christian life-style is guaranteed the growing pains
of struggle, failure, and disappointment. It is not easy. Nothing
truly worthwhile ever is easy. But part of the adventure of
living the Christian life is discovering what God can make of
us.

Now we are children of God, and what we will be has not
yet been made known. But we know that when he appears
we shall be like him, for we shall see him as he is. Everyone
who has this hope in him purifies himself, just as he is
pure (1 John 3:2,3).

All Christians have tremendous untapped potential that God
wants to use for His glory. Developing a Christian life-style
unlocks that potential so we can do things for the Kingdom
beyond our wildest expectations.

PERSONAL SATISFACTION

People simply are happier with themselves and their lives
if their behavior is consistent with their beliefs. God has promised to bless those whose lives conform to His will:

Blessed is the man who does not walk in the counsel of
the wicked or stand in the way of sinners or sit in the seat
of mockers. But his delight is in the law of the Lord, and
on his law he meditates day and night. He is like a tree

planted by streams of water, which yields its fruit in season and whose leaf does not wither. Whatever he does prospers (Psalm 1:1–3).

Job lost everything that was important to him: his wealth, his children, the love of his wife, and the respect of his friends. Yet the Bible says, "In all this, Job did not sin in what he said" (Job 2:10). He remained "blameless and upright, a man who fears God and shuns evil." Job maintained "his integrity" (Job 2:3). Because Job maintained his authentic life-style in the face of severe testing, God blessed him with "twice as much as he had before" (Job 42:10).

Living the Christian life has its own rewards. The satisfaction of having been put to the test and succeeding is tremendous. People who successfully meet a challenge to their Christian life-style are likely to succeed when other challenges come.

The Will of God

Finally, developing a consistent Christian life-style is God's will for the believer. "Do not conform any longer to the pattern of this world, but be transformed by the renewing of your mind. Then you will be able to test and approve what God's will is—his good, pleasing and perfect will" (Romans 12:2).

This transformation from being conformed to the world's pattern to being "conformed to the likeness of his Son" (Romans 8:29) is God's will. And it has always been God's will. Peter quoted the Old Testament (Leviticus 11:44,45) to make that point:

As obedient children, do not conform to the evil desires you had when you lived in ignorance. But just as he who called you is holy, so be holy in all you do; for it is written: "Be holy, because I am holy" (1 Peter 1:14–16).

Holiness has been greatly misunderstood. For many, it is a quaint anachronism, an old-fashioned idea that was good for our grandparents. Others think that if they live 5 years behind the rest of society they are being holy. To some people, holiness is a long list of things Christians do not do, and a person's degree of holiness depends on how many things on the list he does not do.

It is sad that the doctrine of holiness has been so distorted. I am not saying that holiness was not important for our grandparents. It was. But it is not a quaint, old-fashioned idea. Neither does holiness mean living behind the times. I am not saying that Christians ought to keep up with the styles, norms, and values of a pagan society. They should not. And I am certainly not saying that a list of don'ts is necessarily a bad idea. It is not. The church has a responsibility to interact with society and, based on biblical teachings and principles, provide guidance for Christians. Today such teaching is more important than ever.

Holiness is at the core of true Christian living regardless of when or where a believer lives. It means to be like Jesus. How is that possible? Not through human effort or education, but through the supernatural power of God. "If anyone is in Christ, he is a new creation; the old has gone, the new has come!" (2 Corinthians 5:17).

So what difference does a consistent Christian life-style make? All the difference in the world!

NOTES

[1]Robin Burkhart, "Discrepancies Between Belief and Behavior: Implications for Adult Education" (Ann Arbor, Mich.: University Microfilms International, 1987), 115.

[2]Ibid.

4

The Gap

I just could not believe it!

After more than a decade in the pastorate I thought I had heard it all. The minister sees people at their very worst and at the crisis times in their lives. I had dealt with physically and sexually abused children, helped battered women get into safe houses, gone to court with people accused of crimes, helped drug addicts get into rehabilitation, meted out church discipline, and counseled couples whose marriages were falling apart.

It is all in a day's work for a pastor. So her story should not have shocked me. It was like so many others: a marriage in trouble, a husband withdrawn from his wife and children, another woman, and desertion. But as the woman told me her story through agonized sobs, I *was* shocked. She was not an unsaved stranger reaching out to the church in a time of crisis. Nor was her story that of a family on the fringe of the fellowship.

The woman's husband had been the proverbial pillar of the church, a model Christian. The family was faithful in worship, actively involved in ministry, visible around the altars, and in every respect an outstanding example of the Christian family. He was literally the last person I thought would ever turn his back on his family, friends, and faith.

One of the hardest things I have ever had to do is explain to my son why his favorite Sunday school teacher would no longer be there.

"But, Daddy, how could he do that? Wasn't he a Christian?"
Out of the mouths of babes!

We all expect people to live up to what they say they believe. But too often they do not. There is a gap between belief and behavior. And as much as we would like to deny it, we all know that we too are perfectly capable of acting in ways that are contrary to what we believe.

The Gap Between Knowing and Doing

There is no logical and necessary connection between what we know and believe to be true and how we act.[1] Individuals and societies alike are capable of such contradictions.

People who know using tobacco can cause cancer still smoke. People who know drinking and driving can kill still drive drunk. People who know the dangers of high cholesterol still heap on the sour cream and have eggs for breakfast. Such contradictions are all around us.

Jesus knew about the gap. He said, "Now that you know these things, you will be blessed if you do them" (John 13:17). Implicit in that statement are several important insights. First, the plain fact is that it was possible for those listening to Jesus to know the truth and not act accordingly.

Second, it is important to know the truth. It is foolish to think that what people know is not important. Knowledge is the launching pad of behavior.

Third, people are capable of acting contrary to the truth and they do. Many of the Bible's most famous characters failed to act in accordance with the truth. Adam and Eve knew the fruit was forbidden, but they ate it anyway (Genesis 2:15–17; 3:6). Abraham knew that God had promised a son by Sarah, but he slept with Hagar (Genesis 15:5; 16:1–4). David knew his adultery with Bathsheba and the murder of Uriah were sin, but he did them anyway (2 Samuel 11:1–27). The Children of Israel were repeatedly warned about idolatry, but they persisted in the practice (Exodus 20:22,23; 32:1–20). After his rooftop vision,

Peter knew the Gentiles were accepted by God, but he refused to eat with them (Galatians 2:11–14). The list goes on and on.

Fourth, people who consistently act in accordance with what they know will be "blessed" or happy. Consequences follow our actions. If we choose to act in accordance with God's truth, we will experience the blessings and happiness that are the natural result of obedience. But if we choose to disobey, we will experience disastrous consequences. Adam and Eve, David, Abraham, and many other Bible characters had to learn that simple lesson.

> Do not be deceived: God cannot be mocked. A man reaps what he sows. The one who sows to please his sinful nature, from that nature will reap destruction; the one who sows to please the Spirit, from the Spirit will reap eternal life (Galatians 6:7,8).

That is a lesson many today have not learned.

BELIEF/BEHAVIOR RESEARCH

As early as 1928, studies indicated that inconsistencies existed between an individual's beliefs and his or her behavior. Summarizing the results of a study of 11,000 children, one writer stated, "The inconsistency of children was striking; it was impossible to predict, for example, whether a child who cheated on an arithmetic test would also cheat on a spelling test."[2]

In 1934, another study dealt with racial discrimination against Asians. The researcher sought public accommodations at 251 different places while accompanied by a Chinese couple. Only once did that fact prevent him from getting a room. Yet 91 percent of those same establishments replied to a questionnaire that they would not accept Chinese guests.[3]

Many other studies dealing with a wide variety of issues have been conducted over the years. Again and again people were found to act inconsistently with what they said they believed. Studies that have systematically examined the relationship between attitudes and behavior have generally found a lack of correspondence, or at best, a low correspondence between verbally expressed attitudes and overt behavior.[4]

Researchers have offered a number of different explanations for why people do not live up to what they say they believe. Some feel that what people believe is only one factor in the complex equation of behavior. Others feel people are more consistent when what a person knows about an issue corresponds with how he or she feels about it. Self-image, the specific situation, prejudice, the information that is available at the time, the influence of other people, and many other ideas have been advanced to explain why people do not act consistently with what they know and believe.[5]

Some researchers have denied that such inconsistency can really exist. If a person acts contrary to one attitude, it must mean that he acted in accord with another attitude that overrode the first. When there is no consistency between a given attitude and behavior, it is possible there is some other attitude with which the behavior is consistent.[6] According to this view, all behavior is consistent with some belief. To a certain degree, what a person does reveals his true character and what he really believes.

PAUL AND THE BELIEF/BEHAVIOR GAP

The apostle Paul examines the issue of sin in the believer's life in chapters 6, 7, and 8 of Romans. They are rich but controversial chapters with much to teach believers about the Christian life-style.

The believer has a choice in the way he lives. Prior to salvation the believer was a slave to sin (Romans 6:17,20). But through Christ, the power of sin was broken. When "our old self was crucified with him . . . sin [was] rendered powerless, that we should no longer be slaves to sin—because anyone who has died has been freed from sin" (Romans 6:6,7).

While the believer has been freed from sin's dominion, he still has a choice to make.

Don't you know that when you offer yourselves to someone

to obey him as slaves, you are slaves to the one whom you obey—whether you are slaves to sin, which leads to death, or to obedience, which leads to righteousness? (Romans 6:16).

Paul describes the struggle for consistency:

I do not understand what I do. For what I want to do I do not do, but what I hate I do. . . . I have the desire to do what is good, but I cannot carry it out. For what I do is not the good I want to do; no, the evil I do not want to do—this I keep on doing. Now if I do what I do not want to do, it is no longer I who do it, but it is sin living in me that does it. . . .

In my inner being I delight in God's law; but I see another law at work in the members of my body, waging war against the law of my mind and making me a prisoner of the law of sin at work within my members. What a wretched man I am! . . .

So then, I myself in my mind am a slave to God's law, but in the sinful nature a slave to the law of sin (Romans 7:15–25).

Paul eloquently describes the battle for a Christian life-style. Academics may debate the reality of the struggle, but Paul's gripping description leaves little doubt that he agonized over the good he did not do.

The solution to the dilemma is the freedom that is found in Christ. Through Jesus we are set "free from the law of sin and death" (Romans 8:2). Paul divides the world into those controlled by the "sinful nature" and those who live according to the Spirit (Romans 8:5). Those who live according to their sinful nature are controlled by it. Their minds are "set on what that nature desires," are "hostile to God," are unable to "submit to God's law," and "cannot please God" (Romans 8:5–8).

Believers, on the other hand, are to be controlled by the Spirit (Romans 8:9). Because of Christ's work and the Spirit's presence, the believer has an obligation to live according to the Spirit and "put to death the misdeeds of the body" (Romans

8:13). Ultimately, Christian living is found in what Christ has done for the believer, not what the believer has done for Christ.

The Gap and Christian Education

The foremost issues in Christian education are spiritual. While the unbeliever remains under sin's control, the believer has been set free by Christ. Despite that fact, the believer may still choose to obey sin and not God. Helping believers learn to obey God is our task.

Someone once asked the great author Mark Twain if the things in the Bible that he did not understand bothered him. But Twain—like most Christians—recognized that he was not living up to what he already knew about God and the Christian life.

We know far more than we live up to. In fact, we get into trouble most often because we act inconsistently with what we know, not because of what we do not know. With Paul we may exclaim, "What a wretched man I am! Who will rescue me from this body of death?" (Romans 7:24). The answer is the same: "Through Christ Jesus the law of the Spirit of life" sets us "free from the law of sin and death" (Romans 8:2).

Spiritual life is the foundation and essential ingredient of the Christian life-style. Without it there can be no such thing as a Christian life-style. But that does not mean Christian education has no role in the process.

Those of us involved in Christian education should never forget the importance of the Spirit's work in our ministry. No amount of information, teaching, or training will succeed without Him. " 'Not by might nor by power, but by my Spirit,' says the Lord Almighty" (Zechariah 4:6).

My son's Sunday school teacher failed to live up to what he believed. It was his failure and, ultimately, his responsibility. One day he will have to face God with it.

But so will I. My responsibility was to help him become more like Jesus. I was to do everything in my power to encourage his spiritual growth and development. Although his failure was not directly my fault, I cannot help but wonder if I and the rest of his church family did everything we could.

NOTES

[1]Burkhart, "Discrepancies Between Belief and Behavior," 102–174.

[2]Thomas Likona, ed., *Moral Development and Behavior: Theory, Research and Social Issues* (New York: Holt, Rinehart and Winston Pub. Co., 1976), 15.

[3]Richard T. LaPiere, "Attitudes vs. Actions," in *Attitude Theory and Measurement,* ed. Martin Fishbein (New York: John Wiley & Sons, Inc., 1967), 26–31.

[4]M. Rokeach and P. Kleijunas, "Behavior as a Function of Attitude-Toward-Object and Attitude-Toward-Situation," *Journal of Personality and Social Psychology* 22 (1972): 194–201.

[5]Burkhart, "Discrepancies Between Belief and Behavior," 35–55.

[6]Milton Rokeach, *Beliefs, Attitudes and Values: A Theory of Organization and Change* (San Francisco: Jossey-Bass Inc., 1972), 128.

5

At the Core

She was just a young girl, and her question was innocent enough. Even Peter must have been surprised by his own quick and absolute denial of Christ. A man standing by the fire joined in and asked if Peter was a disciple of Jesus. Then, in the flickering firelight, another man recognized Peter as having been with Christ in the Garden.

Peter denied knowing the Lord, cursed, and denied it again. Then he heard the rooster crow (John 18:15–27).

Peter is an enigma. How could the man Jesus had nicknamed the rock—because of his glorious confession of Christ (Matthew 16:13–20)—turn his back on Christ at His moment of greatest need? Didn't Peter believe his own confession? Even harder to understand is the Bible's portrayal of Peter in the Book of Acts (e.g., 2:14–41). How could the coward of the courtyard become the hero of Pentecost?

Peter's experience raises some real questions about the nature of belief and its relationship to behavior. How does what we believe translate into a Christian life-style?

Levels of Belief

The simplest and clearest way to talk about what a person believes is from that person's perspective. People relate to their beliefs in three different ways.[1]

LEVEL #1: BELIEF THAT . . .

At the first level, beliefs are the things a person knows: the facts, bits of information he believes are true or false; a "belief that" something is the case. However, the individual feels little or no personal connection to the facts. To him they are abstract and remote. Belief at this level recognizes something may be true, but does not see it as having any impact on the person.

In the old television series *Dragnet,* Sergeant Joe Friday used to ask for "just the facts." He had no interest in how the people felt about what had happened or how they interpreted its meaning. He wanted only their level #1 beliefs.

Knowing or believing something at this level generally will not lead to action. A person driving at 75 miles per hour on an interstate highway knows the speed limit is 65 miles per hour. He may even believe state troopers are patrolling the highway to enforce the law. But it is not until the driver sees the police car in his rearview mirror and realizes that he may actually get a ticket that he slows down. It is not what the person knows. It is how the person feels the facts affect his or her life.

Are there level #1 Christians? Of course!

"You believe that there is one God. Good! Even the demons believe that—and shudder" (James 2:19). All kinds of people believe in God. They believe that He exists, that He created the universe and is all-knowing. Many even believe in Jesus, but in the same way they believe in any other historical figure. They believe He lived and taught. They may even have great respect for Him, but they have no relationship to Him and no commitment to His cause.

That kind of belief is essential and foundational. Without it there would be no possibility of a deeper and more meaningful belief. But it should never be mistaken for the kind of belief that leads to a Christian life-style.

LEVEL #2: BELIEF IN . . .

At the second level, beliefs are seen as having a direct impact on the person's life. They are the things people "believe in."

Paul posed a dilemma to his Roman readers: "How, then, can they call on the one they have not *believed in?* And how can they *believe in* the one of whom they have not heard?" (Romans 10:14, italics added). The Philippian jailer asked Paul and Silas, " 'What must I do to be saved?' They replied, *'Believe in* the Lord Jesus and you will be saved' " (Acts 16:30,31, italics added).

This level of belief goes beyond accepting something as fact. Millions of people "believe that" Jesus was a historical character. That is not the point. To "believe in" Jesus is to make a decision, a judgment, and a commitment to what you believe is true.

It is easy to illustrate the difference. Most Christians would agree that people who have not accepted Christ as Savior are lost. They would also agree that missionaries should be sent to the unsaved and the church should support their efforts. Someone who "believes that" this statement is true will not necessarily feel any personal responsibility to give to missionary efforts. However, someone who "believes in" the missionary vision will feel that giving is his personal responsibility.

LEVEL #3: I BELIEVE . . .

At the third level of belief the person identifies himself with what he believes. It is the "I believe" level. These beliefs are so connected with the person that they form his self-image. They are the *core values* that guide all of life.

Let's return to our illustration of missionary giving. A person who knows (level #1) and believes (level #2) Christians should give money to missions may or may not give. Whether or not he gives will largely be determined by his self-perception. If he can say, "I believe in missions," he is much more likely to act.

One writer put it this way: "If I believe in something it means that I place myself at the disposal of something, or again that I pledge myself fundamentally, and this pledge affects not only what I have but what I am."[2] It is to commit the total self to act on one's convictions.

Core values function in three ways.[3] First, core values are used to organize one's life and worldview. They determine what is important or trivial and help establish priorities. In making a judgment or evaluating an action, a person must sort through many facts, beliefs, opinions, and ideas. Without core values it would be impossible to make a decision or take an action.

Second, core values have the power to shape one's view of any situation. They help create a perception of oneself, others, the situation, and moral conduct. The same incident will have vastly different meaning for different people, depending on what they value.

Finally, people evaluate morality by their core values. They determine whether an action or attitude is right or wrong. This function makes it possible for people to regard almost anything as good (even Auschwitz), anything as insignificant (even the gospel of Christ), and anything as bad (even the church). It is not that specific moral teaching is not important. It is. But any moral teaching is organized, modified, shaped, and evaluated by core values.

Implications for Christian Education

Our examination of the nature of beliefs points out four very important implications for Christian education. First, it is critically important to recognize that all beliefs are not held in the same way. Just knowing something or believing it is true does not mean a person will respond appropriately. The issue is not what a person knows, but his connection to what he knows.

Understanding that truth gives us a sense of the progression Christian education should take. God's Word must be taught so the student not only accepts it as true, but also commits himself to it. Beyond that, Christian education must lead to an identification of the self with the truth of God's Word. Christian education must challenge the student to respond to the claims of the gospel and identify with Christ.

"As he thinketh [estimates the value] in his heart, so is he" (Proverbs 23:7, KJV). What a man values at the core of his being makes him what he is. This view of belief may be visualized as three rings with the same center. At the center are a person's core values. Around the core values are the things the person believes in, and around both are the things the person believes are true.

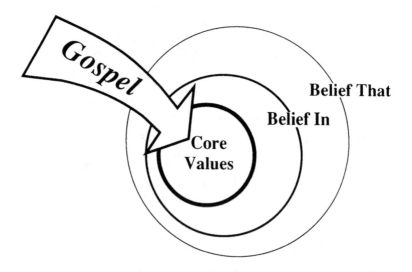

The message of Christ comes from outside ourselves and must penetrate the first ring so the person knows about Jesus. Then it must penetrate the next ring so the person puts his trust in Jesus as his Savior. Finally, the gospel must reach the core of the person's being so he identifies life itself with Christ. That is the task of Spirit-filled Christian education.

Second, we must ask what kind of education our learners experience in Sunday school. Are they helped to move from "belief that" to "I believe"? Much of what we do in Christian education is focused at the most fundamental level. We want our students to *know* what the Bible says and the church teaches. However, some people know what the Bible says and are just as lost as those who have never heard the gospel.

Third, this view of belief and behavior challenges us to ask,

"Is it possible for educational experiences to help learners move to the 'I believe' level and develop a truly Christian life-style?" I believe it is. But one thing is certain: No educational method can achieve that aim without the Holy Spirit's power and presence.

Finally, this view challenges our understanding of the relationship between belief and behavior. Traditionally people have thought of that relationship as a straight line.

KNOWLEDGE ♦ ATTITUDE ♦ ACTION

However, the belief-behavior relationship is more accurately seen in the following illustration.

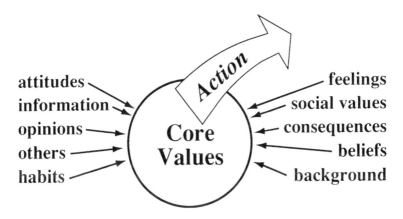

At the center of life are core values. In any situation many factors have to be considered. All the factors are evaluated and prioritized, and from their mix springs action. The controlling factor in the process is the core value; what is most important to the person making the decision. Christian education's role is to help the learner develop a commitment to the gospel and the cause of Christ as the most important priority.

In Matthew 16:13–15, Jesus asked Peter two questions: "Who

do people say the Son of Man is?" and "Who do you say I am?" Christ's first question asked Peter for the facts. Peter's first response represented level #1 beliefs. He reported his "belief that" others viewed Christ in various ways. But his second response, "You are the Christ," revealed that Peter "believed in" Jesus.

On one of His last days on earth, Jesus asked Peter another question three times. " 'Simon son of John, do you love me?' " Three times Peter answered, " 'Yes, Lord, you know that I love you.' " After Peter's response, Jesus told Peter to feed and take care of His sheep (John 21:15–17). Jesus made a connection between Peter's identification with Christ and what he should do.

The transformation from the coward of the courtyard to the hero of Pentecost resulted from two crucial factors: Peter's identification with Christ and the Day of Pentecost. The two must always go together. Believers must fully identify with Christ and the gospel and also "receive power when the Holy Spirit comes" upon them (Acts 1:8). Christian living will be the outcome.

NOTES

[1]Burkhart, "Discrepancies Between Belief and Behavior," 15–16.

[2]G. Marcel, *The Mystery of Being, Part II* (Chicago: Henry Regnery Press Co., 1960), 77.

[3]Burkhart, "Discrepancies Between Belief and Behavior," 186–190.

6

Practice Makes Perfect: Closing the Gap Between Belief and Behavior

Listen to my tale
Of Jonah and the whale,
Way down in the middle of the ocean,
How did he get there,
Whatever did he wear?
Way down in the middle of the ocean;
Preaching he should be
At Ninevah you see,
He disobeyed!
A very foolish notion!
But God forgave his sin,
Salvation enter'd in,
Way down in the middle of the ocean.[1]

Do you remember singing that little chorus in Sunday school? The prophet Jonah is an interesting example of a person who did not live up to what he believed. He was God's prophet, called to preach repentance to the people of Ninevah. But he hated the Ninevites and knew if he went and preached they would repent and God would spare them. So he booked passage on a ship headed in the opposite direction. A great storm and a great fish intervened and Jonah found himself "way down in the middle of the ocean."

Inside the fish, Jonah had time to reconsider God's offer. He decided he would rather preach in Ninevah than be digested by the fish. Back on dry land, God called him again and this time Jonah obeyed. As a result of Jonah's preaching, the people of Ninevah did repent. God sent a great revival and spared the city. Jonah finally was where God wanted him, doing God's work. But what a way to get there!

The Process

In Jonah's life we see a process of closing the gap between belief and behavior. What are the steps people need to take to resolve the differences between what they believe they should be and what they are? Research has identified a four-step process: (a) awareness, (b) deliberation, (c) decision, and (d) action.[2]

AWARENESS

How can people act inconsistently with what they say they believe and not be aware they are doing so? Knowing that belief and behavior do not match is not the same as being aware of a discrepancy. Awareness is the crystallization of the discrepancy into something that must be dealt with.

People may act contrary to their beliefs and not be aware of it for a number of different reasons. First, they may be genuinely ignorant of what they should or should not do. It is possible to be very committed to Christ and not know that a specific action or attitude is contrary to Christ's teachings. For example, a new Christian may not pay tithes simply because he is unaware of the believer's obligation to support the church. His behavior is inconsistent because of ignorance.

Second, a person may be unaware of his inconsistency because he fails to make the connection between the abstract teachings of Christ and his daily living. He does not see how what he believes applies in a specific situation. Someone may know about tithing, but not apply that teaching to his own finances.

Finally, people rationalize. They are aware of what they should do, but feel justified in not doing it. A believer facing financial pressure may feel perfectly justified in not paying his tithes. It is easy in that situation to rationalize the discrepancy away by saying he cannot afford to tithe, or he needs to pay his bills first, or he has to meet his family's needs.

If a person is to deal with behavior that does not live up to belief he must first be aware that a discrepancy exists. Sources of this awareness are internal and external.

Internal Sources of Awareness

Conscience, our internal sense of right and wrong, is a source of awareness. It is our moral guidance system and its purpose is to bear witness to the law of God that is written on everyone's heart (Romans 2:15; 9:1). The function of the conscience is to convict the individual of right and wrong.

The Bible describes two kinds of consciences. The good conscience is turned toward God (1 Peter 3:21), is clear before God and man (Acts 24:16; Hebrews 13:18), and is consistent with the faith (1 Timothy 1:19). The evil conscience is unbelieving (Titus 1:15) and seared (1 Timothy 4:1,2). Those with seared consciences are "hypocritical liars." The evil conscience cannot distinguish between what is right and what is wrong.

The conscience is formed. The good conscience is shaped by the Holy Spirit, while the evil conscience is seared by sin. The fact that people exhibit different levels of sensitivity to the same issue demonstrates that the conscience is formed. The Bible talks about those with a weak conscience as those who are more sensitive than others (1 Corinthians 8:7).

The author of Hebrews describes the process by which the believer can be cleansed "from a guilty conscience" (Hebrews 10:22). First, he must recognize that only the blood of Jesus cleanses the conscience (9:14). The believer is to "draw near to God with a sincere heart in full assurance of faith" (10:22).

The second internal source of awareness is self-examination. The Christian is told to examine and judge himself (1 Corinthians 11:28,31). Beyond self-examination, believers are called on to test their faith (2 Corinthians 13:5) and their actions (Galatians 6:4). But self-examination must be linked to the Psalmist's prayer: "Search me, O God, and know my heart; test me and know my anxious thoughts. See if there is any offensive way in me, and lead me in the way everlasting" (Psalm 139:23,24).

The Holy Spirit is the third internal source of awareness. His work is to

> convict the world of guilt in regard to sin and righteousness and judgment; in regard to sin, because men do not believe in me; in regard to righteousness, because I am going to the Father, where you can see me no longer; and in regard to judgment, because the prince of this world stands condemned (John 16:8–11).

External Sources of Awareness

Other people can be a source of awareness through confrontation and shared personal experiences. Nathan confronted David with his sin with Bathsheba (2 Samuel 12) and brought about David's repentance. Paul confronted Peter with his hypocrisy when he refused to eat with Gentile believers (Galatians 2:11–14). God commanded Ezekiel to confront men with their sin and warn them of His judgment (Ezekiel 3:18–20).

A second external source of awareness is a personal experience or crisis that crystallizes the discrepancy. Peter's experience with the Gentiles at Cornelius' house when they received the baptism in the Holy Spirit made the other disciples aware of their failure to fulfill the Great Commission and take the gospel to the Gentiles.

Information is the third external source of awareness. New information confronts old assumptions. Peter's vision of clean and unclean animals (Acts 10:9–23) challenged His Jewish prejudice against Gentiles. Without a doubt, Peter believed he had been acting consistently with God's will by focusing on the Jews and not the Gentiles. After all, Jesus had said He was sent "to the lost sheep of Israel" (Matthew 15:24). But Peter had been acting inconsistently with the Great Commission (Matthew 28:19) and the vision made him aware of it.

The fourth and final external source of awareness is a personal crisis. In a time of crisis, people often are confronted with their failure to live up to what they say they believe. Jonah was on his way to Tarshish, Paul was on his way to Damascus, and David was in his palace when each was confronted with his inconsistency. The force of such experiences can bring dormant discrepancies to the surface.

DELIBERATION

The second step a person must take to resolve an inconsistency is deliberation. Once aware that he is not living up to his beliefs, the individual must decide what to do about it. During this period of deliberation the person asks, "How can I make it right?" or, "How do I change it?" The process of deliberation has two parts: the search and evaluation.

The Search

After being confronted with an inconsistency in his life, the person begins a search for information, advice, and support. He looks for resources that can help him overcome the discrepancy and achieve the desired change in his life. He wants to know his options, what others have done in similar circumstances, and what kind of backing he will get from the people who are important to him.

Evaluation

In evaluating a discrepancy, the person is concerned with whether or not it is really important. Some discrepancies may be considered so unimportant that they are ignored and the process ends. The person also analyzes the different ways the discrepancy could be resolved and the consequences of each. Finally, he takes a long, hard look at his values, principles, and self-image.

DECISION

At some point, the person experiencing the discrepancy has

to make up his mind. The decision step has three distinct parts. First, the person must set a course of action. In setting the course of action he must not only choose what he will do, but also set aside other possible solutions. Next, he must commit himself to that course of action. He must count the cost and determine to follow through.

Finally, the person has to want to resolve the discrepancy. A person can be aware of a discrepancy, ponder his future, and decide on a course of action. But if he is not motivated to change, the process ends.

ACTION

The final step in the process is action. A person must take the plunge to resolve the discrepancy. If the process does not lead to action, it has failed. Action of this kind will ultimately demand effort, discipline, and perseverance. Changes are not immediate or easy, and they demand great sacrifice and persistence.

This process is illustrated in the life of the rich young ruler (Luke 18:18–29). He came to Jesus with an important question and got more than he bargained for. He wanted to know what he had to do "to inherit eternal life." He must have been thrilled when Christ replied that he should keep the commandments. He had kept them from his youth.

But the second part of Christ's response unsettled the young man: " 'Sell everything you have and give to the poor, and you will have treasure in heaven. Then come, follow me' " (Luke 18:22). The Bible tells us the young man went away "very sad, because he was a man of great wealth" (18:23).

Jesus presented the rich young ruler with a true dilemma. If he was serious about obtaining eternal life he would have to make following Jesus, not his wealth, the most important thing in his life.

In this passage, we find the process of resolving inconsistencies sharply focused. Jesus made the rich young ruler aware of the discrepancy in his life: You cannot love God and money because no man can serve two masters (Luke 16:13). Then the young man deliberated and decided how to clear up his dilemma. Finally, he took action. He turned his back on Jesus and turned to his wealth.

Implications for Christian Education

What are the implications of the way people close the gaps between belief and behavior?

THE SUNDAY SCHOOL AND AWARENESS

The Sunday school can assist the believer in developing his internal sources of awareness. It can contribute to the conscience by clearly declaring what the Bible teaches. It can challenge the believer to evaluate his life in light of the Scriptures. Finally, the Sunday school can provide a spiritual atmosphere in which the Holy Spirit can work in the believer's life.

The Sunday school can also provide external sources of awareness. By faithfully presenting what the Bible teaches, the Sunday school can help create a new vision of what the Christian life should be. The Sunday school can also be a place of personal experience where the individual is challenged to act like a Christian and is confronted with other people who are also struggling to live the Christian life. Finally, the Sunday school should be a caring environment where students going through a crisis can find guidance, help, and support.

THE SUNDAY SCHOOL AND DELIBERATION

In the Sunday school class setting, people can search for more information and seek advice and support. They can evaluate how they are living in the context of a loving, supportive group of people. The class provides an opportunity for the individual to explore the consequences of his present life-style, biblical principles, and possible changes. Finally, the Sunday school should be a place where the desire to be like Jesus is created and nurtured.

THE SUNDAY SCHOOL AND DECISION

Following the examination of God's Word, the teacher should find ways to challenge the learners to decide what they are going to do about the truth they have studied. It is a question that should be asked in some form in every Sunday school class.

THE SUNDAY SCHOOL AND ACTION

It is not enough to ask people what they are going to do about God's truth. The Sunday school should create opportunities to put it into practice. Teachers should consciously look for ways to take action during the class. For example, a study of prayer should certainly include a time when the students pray. A study of the baptism in the Holy Spirit should give the students an opportunity to seek the experience. A lesson on sharing should provide an opportunity for the students to share.

But that is not enough. Sunday school class members should be acting on God's truth outside the classroom. Learners should be given the opportunity to share how they applied last week's lesson with their friends. Beyond that the teacher should plan events when the class does the work of the ministry together. Such class ministry should not be seen as a nice extra if there is time and opportunity, but as an essential part of the teaching/learning process.

Jonah finally obeyed God's command and conformed his behavior to his belief. But after the revival, Jonah became depressed because God forgave the people of Ninevah and did not destroy them. So he built a lean-to on the side of a hill and sat and sulked.

A vine grew up and gave Jonah shade, but God sent a worm to kill the plant. Jonah grew angry and complained to God about the heat. Again God confronted Jonah with not living up to what he believed (Jonah 4).

Becoming more like Jesus is a lifelong process for the believer. Christian education has a vital role to play. The only question is whether or not we will do it.

NOTES

[1]Hugh Mitchell, comp., *Zondervan's Sunbeam Songs for Boys and Girls Volume One* (Grand Rapids, Mich.: Zondervan, 1957), 7.

[2]Burkhart, "Discrepancies Between Belief and Behavior," 162–172.

7

The kN.E.A.R. Principle: The Elements of Life-Style Education

The story of Christ's encounter with Zacchaeus is found in Luke 19:1–9. Zacchaeus must have been miserable. As the chief tax collector, he was the agent of the occupying Roman government and collaborator with the enemy. Beyond that, he had apparently used his power to cheat the people and become very wealthy. He is the picture of a corrupt, greedy, and unhappy little man.

Several things happened to Zacchaeus the day Jesus saw him in the sycamore tree. First, Zacchaeus gladly welcomed Jesus into his house. Second, Jesus established a relationship with Zacchaeus by going to his house and spending time with him. Third, Zacchaeus recognized Jesus as his Lord. Finally, Zacchaeus changed. He promised to give half of what he owned to the poor and repay anyone he had cheated (Luke 19:5–8).

The story has a happy ending. After Zacchaeus made his announcement, Jesus said, " 'Today salvation has come to this house, because this man, too, is a son of Abraham. For the Son of Man came to seek and to save what was lost' " (Luke 19:9).

Salvation came not because Zacchaeus gave to the poor and paid back what he had stolen. He gave to the poor and paid back what he had stolen because salvation had come. Salvation came to Zacchaeus as it does to every other sinner: through faith and trust in Jesus as God's Son.

The encounter between Zacchaeus and Jesus illustrates a principle of life-style education that I call the kN.E.A.R. principle. Four key elements make up this principle: (a) Knowledge, (b) Emotions, (c) Action, and (d) Relationships. These four elements are always part of a life-changing educational event. They must be incorporated into our Sunday schools if we are to help people be like Jesus.

Knowledge

Knowledge is the first critical element of life-style education. Zacchaeus came to know and understand that Jesus was much more than a traveling rabbi. He was the Christ, the Son of the living God, the Messiah. More important, Zacchaeus came to know Jesus as his Lord.

Our Sunday schools must be concerned with what people know. In discussing the various views of the Sunday school in chapter 1, we looked at three important areas of understanding: (1) what the Bible teaches, (2) what the church understands, and (3) how that understanding is to be applied in the believer's life. The Bible is and must be the Sunday school's text. Sunday school curriculum, resource materials, and other tools are subordinate to the Bible.

Here we want to talk about the impact of what believers know on their life-style and on the educational process. What people know does have an impact on what they do and how they live. Research indicates that consistency between attitudes and behavior will increase with an increase in the amount and accuracy of the available information.[1]

The fact that people can and do act contrary to what they know to be the truth does not mean that what they know and understand is not important to them. Knowledge is one of the basic building blocks of a life-style. People act differently depending on what they know about a given situation. We all make decisions and act based on what we know at the time. Later we may regret a decision or an action and wish that we had done something else. Not having enough information or having misinformation may have disastrous results.

A few years ago, my wife and I visited Pearl Harbor and

several other sights connected with December 7, 1941. We were especially interested because our fathers had passed through Pearl on their way to duty in the South Pacific during World War II. We stood on the *U.S.S. Arizona* memorial and looked down into the waters of Pearl Harbor at the rusting grave of 1,000 sailors.

I was surprised to learn that the Japanese had flown from north to south across the island before attacking the ships. They had been spotted by radar and observed by civilians, but everyone had assumed they were overdue American planes.

That misinformation had disastrous results for the American Navy that Sunday morning. I could not help but wonder if the radar operators had had better information, things would have turned out differently. Not knowing and understanding what the Bible teaches can have an equally disastrous impact on the believer's life.

Contrary to the old saying, what a person does not know can hurt him. Not knowing what the Bible teaches may lead to several disastrous results. First, it may lead to outright disobedience of God's laws. Second, such ignorance makes the believer vulnerable to deception. The cults are full of people from churched backgrounds who did not know enough about the Bible to defend themselves against the cults' lies. Ignorant believers are also vulnerable to satanic deception. They, like Eve, may be tricked into disobedience. The antidote to deception is a knowledge of God's Word.

Finally, the ignorant believer may be deprived of the rights and privileges that belong to God's children. If the believer does not know the baptism in the Holy Spirit is part of his birthright, he will be deprived of its blessing. If he does not know he is gifted by the Spirit for ministry, he will be deprived of the blessing of service. Again, the antidote is for the Sunday school to teach the full gospel.

Emotions

Jesus had an emotional impact on Zacchaeus: "[Zacchaeus]

came down at once and welcomed him gladly" (Luke 19:6). The pure joy and excitement that Zacchaeus experienced must have been staggering. He was the pariah of the city, rejected and condemned by his neighbors. But Jesus, the most famous and loved rabbi of the day, wanted to go to his house. There is no doubt the emotional impact of this encounter affected Zacchaeus' decision to follow Christ.

Again, we have already discussed the importance of developing biblically correct attitudes and values and the importance of experiencing God's power and presence. Here, as with our discussion of knowledge, we want to look at the impact of emotions on life-style education. How people feel about God, the Bible, the church, and other believers is a key element in the educational event. Any Sunday school that wants to help people develop an authentically Christian life-style must consider its emotional impact.

First, emotions can reinforce or cancel what was learned. If a person has a positive feeling about the learning experience he is more likely to accept and act on what was taught. However, if he has a strong negative reaction to the educational experience he is likely to reject the teaching along with the teacher and the church.

Second, emotions are important because they represent basic human needs. An educational experience that meets those needs will have a greater impact than one that ignores them.

Third, emotions are the gateway to the mind. They can open a person to learning he would otherwise reject. If a person's emotional needs for love and acceptance are met, he is more likely to hear and accept what is being taught. It has long been the strategy of the cults to show people love and acceptance. Once the individual is made part of the family he is ripe for indoctrination.

Finally, emotions shape our perception of what we know. What we know cannot be separated from the emotional setting in which it was learned. Every educational experience has an emotional impact that directly affects learning.

People not only need to know what God's Word says, they

also need to feel good about God, His Word, and His church. That too is the Sunday school's job.

Action

Zacchaeus responded to Christ with clear, decisive action. He gave half of his wealth to the poor and to those from whom he had stolen he gave back four times what he had taken.

Action has real value in the educational process. Attitudes formed by direct personal interaction result in greater consistency between belief and behavior.[2] Not only is belief an integral part of action, but action is an integral part of the development, testing, and crystallization of belief.[3]

Actions that do not match beliefs can create the conditions for the reassessment and revision of those beliefs and set in motion the process of change. Change in belief most often results from the presence of an inconsistency. One of the ways this state of imbalance occurs is when a person engages in an action that is not compatible with his beliefs.[4]

A change in behavior is more likely to result in a change in attitude, rather than a change in attitude resulting in a change in behavior.[5] The relationship between attitude and action is a continuing, reciprocal, and circular process.[6]

Clearly an educational scheme that intends to help people develop a Christian life-style must consciously include an emphasis on Christian behavior. Action not only reinforces what has been learned, but also creates a situation in which beliefs that are contrary to Christian behavior can be examined, evaluated, and changed.

Jesus consciously included action in His disciples' training. He sent out the Seventy to do the work of the ministry (Luke 10:1,17, KJV). They returned "with joy" after a successful trip. This on-the-job training had a strong impact on the disciples' lives. Learning by doing was also a standard part of Paul's training of Timothy, Silas, and John Mark.

Relationships

Recently much has been made of the Sunday school teacher as a model. Being a model and having a personal relationship with the learner are two very different things. A model may be viewed from a distance and requires no personal involvement. Of course, Sunday school teachers should be good models, but that is not enough. They should also develop close personal relationships with their learners if they hope to help them develop an authentic Christian life-style.

Jesus was the perfect model for Zacchaeus to follow. Zacchaeus had clearly admired Jesus before their meeting that day. But his behavior did not change until Jesus chose to have a personal relationship with him.

The importance of relationships is emphasized in the Scriptures. Jesus formed a close relationship with His disciples and, over the years they were together, the disciples formed close relationships with each other. It is interesting to note that Jesus may have been a model for the multitudes, but He was a friend to the Twelve. This example was copied by Barnabas, who took the newly converted Paul under his wing. Later, Paul built strong relationships with John Mark, Silas, Timothy, and others.

Strong relationships in the Sunday school classroom provide essential elements for life-style education. The Sunday school class provides an opportunity for greater awareness of the Christian life as lived through other believers. It should be a place where people feel secure in their relationships and can explore ways to be more like Jesus. Finally, it ought to provide the support and encouragement so necessary for Christian growth and development.

With this understanding of the basics of life-style education, we will look at how they should be applied and practiced in the Sunday school classroom. Applying them takes hard work, but in the end it will really pay off in the lives of our learners.

Knowledge and the Sunday School

What informational resources are available to the Sunday school as it endeavors to communicate the gospel?

CURRICULUM RESOURCES

The first and most basic informational resource for the Sunday school is the Bible. Nothing can or should replace it. But, in most cases, teachers have the added resource of Bible-based instructional material or curriculum. Good material should have the following characteristics.

Biblical

Sunday school curriculum should be faithful to the Bible. If it lacks this quality, regardless of its other strengths, it cannot be considered good Sunday school curriculum.

Sound Doctrine

Christians of different traditions hotly disagree over a number of important issues. Each tradition claims its particular understanding is biblically correct. It is important, therefore, that the Sunday school material and the church speak with one voice on such issues.

Age-Level Sensitivity

People of different ages have different abilities and needs. The better the match between the learners' needs and abilities and the resource material, the more likely it is that the students will actually learn.

Learning-Style Sensitivity

People learn in different ways. Ideally, each learner would be able to study God's Word in his preferred style. But that is not practical or possible in the classroom. Resource material, however, can provide a wide variety of activities and approaches that allow learners with different learning styles to participate.

Scope and Sequence

Sunday school material should build "precept upon precept; line upon line" (Isaiah 28:13, KJV). As a student attends week after week and year after year, each lesson should build on what was taught before. The failure to coordinate what is taught and build over time is a major weakness of teacher-produced material and of the Sunday school that uses material from different sources.

Application

Good Sunday school material guides the teacher and the student to apply the lesson in everyday life.

User-Friendly

The material should be easy for the teacher to use and for the student to understand.

HUMAN RESOURCES

The second crucial resource in the classroom is the teacher. The teacher is the single most critical element in the formula. To a large degree, the teacher controls everything that happens in the classroom. Good teachers can teach under the worst conditions. Bad teachers cannot teach under the best.

What makes a good Sunday school teacher? All great Sunday school teachers demonstrate two important qualities.

Prayerful

The effective Sunday school teacher has planned to be effective. He has invested the time and effort to make sure everything needed for a quality educational event has been done.

Prepared

The effective Sunday school teacher is prepared with a good lesson plan and everything needed to make the plan work, skills enhanced by training, and goals developed through prayer, Bible study, and the Holy Spirit's guidance.

Emotions and the Sunday School

The physical and attitudinal environments are powerful emotional factors.

PHYSICAL ENVIRONMENT

Several important factors should be taken into account when considering the Sunday school's physical environment. Among them are (1) room size, (2) decor, (3) temperature, (4) furnishings, (5) cleanliness, and (6) equipment and supplies.

ATTITUDINAL ENVIRONMENT

The attitudinal environment is every bit as important as the physical environment. No beautifully equipped classroom can make up for an unfriendly atmosphere. But a loving and caring atmosphere can make up for a less-than-perfect room.

People can sense when they are sincerely loved and cared about. The teacher can make sure the students are given the opportunity to build friendly, loving relationships with each other during the class.

The Sunday school class should be a positive place. Again, it begins with the teacher's attitude. The teacher should feel that ministry in the Sunday school is a privilege. He should be genuinely happy to see his students and should do everything in his power to ensure that the attitudinal environment is positive.

Finally, the teacher can make sure the class is emotionally safe by protecting the members from other students' unkind or insensitive words and actions. Each person needs to feel he can share his feelings and ideas without being laughed at, ridiculed, or otherwise put down by the teacher or other students.

Action and the Sunday School

Behavior, or action, is an integral part of the Sunday school experience both inside and outside the classroom.

The Sunday school classroom is an ideal place to put beliefs into practice. Each lesson should involve some active learning and practicing the skills and principles learned that Sunday. It should also include the opportunity to reflect on how previous lessons were applied in the students' daily lives.

Ultimately the lessons of Scripture need to be practiced outside the classroom. The students should make them a part of their everyday life. Teachers can do little more than encourage their students to apply the lessons at home, at work, or at school. However, class projects and ministry involvement can provide opportunities for the students to act on what they have learned. Good teachers will regularly plan such activities in their classes.

Relationships and the Sunday School

One of the most vivid images of the church is that of a loving family in which God is our Father, Christ is our older Brother, and we are all brothers and sisters. We used to emphasize the family quality of the church by calling each other "brother" or "sister." The Sunday school class ought to be an extension of that spiritual family. As such, it always involves three vital relationships: the student and the teacher, the students with each other, and the student and God.

The teacher/student relationship should reflect the unique characteristics of the church as the family of God. If the teacher expects his students to hear what he has to say, he must build a trusting and mutually supportive friendship with them. Like Jesus, the Sunday school teacher must be a personal friend inside and outside the classroom.

While often overlooked, the relationship the learners have

with other learners may be just as important as the relationship they have with their teacher. In some cases, it may be even more significant. Teachers need to be sensitive to this fact and try to create opportunities for their learners to develop healthy relationships.

The most important relationship in the Sunday school classroom is between the student and God. Each student must develop his own spiritual walk, and no one, including the Sunday school teacher, can do it for him.

The Sunday school should be the laboratory of the Holy Spirit. Through times of prayer and worship, as well as study, the student should experience God's presence. While developing a close relationship with God must be the individual believer's daily concern, the Sunday school class can greatly enhance and encourage that development.

NOTES

[1]Andrew R. Davidson, Steven Yantis, Marel Norwood, and Daniel E. Montano, "Amount of Information About the Attitude-Object and Attitude-Behavior Consistency," *Journal of Personality and Social Psychology* 49 (1985): no. 5, 1184–1198.

[2]D.T. Regan and R. Fazio, "On the Consistency Between Attitudes and Behavior: Look to the Method of Attitude Formation," *Journal of Experimental Social Psychology* 13 (1977): 28–45.

[3]Herbert C. Kelman, "Attitudes Are Alive and Well and Gainfully Employed in the Sphere of Action," *American Psychologist* 29 (1974): 324.

[4]Ibid, 321–324.

[5]C.A. Insko and J. Schopler, "Triadic Consistency: A Statement of Affective-Cognitive-Conative Consistency," *Psychological Review* 74 (1967): no. 5, 361–376.

[6]Kelman, "Attitudes Are Alive and Well," 310–324.

8

Life-Style Education for Preschool and Elementary Children

One of my favorite mental images of Jesus is a scene where people were bringing their little children to Him so He could touch them. The disciples rebuked them, but when Jesus saw what was going on He became indignant with the disciples and said, " 'Let the little children come to me, and do not hinder them, for the kingdom of God belongs to such as these.' " Then "he took the children in his arms, put his hands on them and blessed them" (Mark 10:13–16).

We do not know why the disciples objected to the parents bringing their children to Jesus. Perhaps they thought He was too busy or that He had more important things to do. But Jesus wanted the children close to Him. They were important in the Kingdom and important to Him. Little children ought to be that important to the church today. Unfortunately, some in the church act more like the disciples than like Jesus.

Catching a Life-Style

Perhaps the preschool stage of life can be best described as catching a life-style. The young child is plunged into a world in which he has little or no control. He cannot choose his parents, his siblings, his home, or his church. Nevertheless, he is forced to deal with all those factors to make sense out of his world. These early days of life have a profound impact on the rest of life.

Anne Ortland wrote a book called *Children Are Wet Cement.*[1] While that is not a flattering image of childhood, her main idea is worth considering: Like wet cement, children are easily marked, and those marks can become permanent.

That image, however, should not be taken too far. Children, even young children, are not passively waiting for someone else to shape their lives. Each person inherits unique qualities and responds differently to his environment. Young children are people actively responding to the experiences of life.

On the other hand, there is a sense in which young children are like wet cement. What happens during their early years can permanently mark their lives. The impressions of God formed in those early days can set a person on the road to accepting or rejecting God. Christian educators must be very careful about the kind of impression they make. It may have eternal consequences.

The Preschool Learner

Wes Haystead has identified different ways preschool children acquire information, including through their senses, repetition, experience, play, imitation, and connecting words and actions. Preschoolers tend to process that information according to the past, from a self-centered point of view, and with a concrete interpretation.[2]

Keith and Sharon Drury have identified characteristics of preschoolers as learners.[3] Physically, the children are bundles of energy. Since they are developing at different rates, children of the same age in the same class may have vastly different abilities. All their senses are important to them, not just sight and sound. The lack of small-muscle development makes skilled and detailed activities difficult and frustrating.

Emotionally, preschoolers are walking contradictions. On the one hand, they may be fearful and very shy. On the other, they may be silly and boisterous. Socially, they are egocentric and see everything in terms of self. *Bossy* is another word that may describe them. Preschoolers can also be very social and enjoy the company of their peers. Finally, they are fiercely independent and at the same time very dependent. They desperately want to do things on their own, but they still need a great deal of help.

Intellectually, the children are curious, full of questions, and imaginative. But they are limited in their understanding and ability to deal with concepts. Since they think of everything in concrete terms, abstract ideas are difficult for them to grasp. Finally, they have a short attention span. An attention span is the length of time a person can concentrate on one item. While attention spans vary with each child, a good rule of thumb is 1 minute per each year of life.

Preschoolers have an awakening spirituality and are able to learn spiritual truths. Of course, their spiritual insight is very different from that of older children and adults. But adults can learn much from the simple beauty of childlike spirituality. Jesus said, " 'I tell you the truth, anyone who will not receive the kingdom of God like a little child will never enter it' " (Mark 10:15).

CENTER STAGE

Those who work with young children should be concerned about their knowledge, emotions, actions, and relationships. Goals developed for any age-level should reflect these priorities. However, at different age-levels different areas take center stage. It is not that the others are unimportant. But each age presents unique opportunities for spiritual development. Educators should be sensitive to those opportunities and take advantage of them.

For preschool children, emotions are at center stage. James Michael Lee states that the Sunday school should deliberately and consciously teach attitudes, employing concrete firsthand experiences and interpersonal interaction targeted toward values.[4]

Lucie Barber asserts that preschool education in the church

ought to focus on learning foundational attitudes and values.[5] She emphasizes three attitudes: faith, hope, and love.

Barber defines faith in terms of trust in the dependability of those who love and care for the child, an appreciation for nature, and the predictability of events. Hope is seen as reliance on the kingdom of God now and in the hereafter, and a trust in God's greater knowledge and understanding. Barber sees love in terms of developing a positive self-regard and a positive orientation toward others. The child should develop these attitudes in terms of the Bible, prayer, the church as a community, the church in worship, and the Sunday school.

The Sunday school's ability to impact the other areas of life will be determined largely by the learner's attitudes and values. The Sunday school can help preschool learners get off to a good start by focusing on these issues. Creating a firm foundation of faith, hope, and love is the preschool Sunday school teacher's task. Others will build on that foundation.

Life-Style Education and the Young Child

How should the principles of life-style education be applied to the young child? What are the best ways to meet his needs and abilities?

KNOWLEDGE

Preschool children need to know what the Bible teaches. But that information must come to them in a suitable form. First, it must be at their level. A single year of life can make a vast difference in a child's development. Next, biblical information should be given in small capsules, which are best presented in the form of Bible and life-application stories. The stories should be kept simple with a minimum of detail, and the point of the story must be clearly in focus.

The Bible story should be the focus of conversation and activity for the session. Activities should be planned to reinforce the story's content and the lesson it was intended to teach. The teacher should engage the children in conversation about the story and the lesson. The preschoolers should be encouraged to ask questions and talk about the lesson and its meaning to them.

EMOTIONS

The teacher should be especially sensitive to the students' emotional needs. First, and most important, young children need to feel safe. Leaving the security of the family and going to a strange place with strangers can be a terrifying experience for anyone. Everything possible should be done to help relieve the child's fears.

The teacher should make a special effort to help the preschoolers feel loved, accepted, and important. He should greet the children by name as they arrive, listen to their stories, and demonstrate genuine affection. Appropriate facilities, equipment, and enough supplies to go around will help the children feel they are important.

ACTION

Preschoolers are active learners with very short attention spans. They need a variety of fast-paced activities. Music, drama, coloring, playing house, building with blocks, and making things with clay are just a few of the activities that help the young child learn. Good Sunday school material will provide an almost endless supply of ideas. Such activities should be used every Sunday.

RELATIONSHIPS

The teacher must build loving and trusting relationships with the students. This requires several very important steps. First, the children need to see the same faces week after week. While adults may appreciate teaching only once every month or quarter, a constant stream of strangers can be frightening for young children.

Second, the teacher must establish a relationship with the

child in and out of the classroom. It is important that the children see the teacher as a friend, not a remote authority figure. However, the teacher needs to establish control. Teacher control in the preschool classroom is not contrary to building a close relationship, but an essential part of that relationship.

Teacher-student ratios are critical to building strong relationships and making sure the children have a positive experience in Sunday school. There should be no more than five preschool children for each adult in the classroom. A larger number of children prevents the teacher from giving each child the individualized attention he needs. It makes control very difficult, and Sunday morning may become an unpleasant experience for both the teacher and the child.

Jesus stopped what He was doing and took the time to touch and hold the little ones who were brought to Him. In that simple act, He was the ideal model of a preschool Sunday school teacher. He loved the children and met their needs. So should we.

Conforming to a Life-Style

In any Sunday school class are future pastors, missionaries, board members, political and business leaders, parents, and Sunday school teachers. We simply do not know who will turn out to be what. Frequently adults feel ambivalent about children. We are excited about their potential, but often frustrated by their behavior.

Perhaps this stage of life can best be thought of as that time when we conform to a life-style. Family, friends, the neighborhood, school, and church largely determine the elementary child's life-style. Life is not a matter of choosing how one will live, but of fitting into the life around him. In that process, a person forms much of his self-identity and value system. Some people are fortunate enough to be born into homes that nurture a healthy self-image and attitudes. Others struggle in homes that destroy rather than build.

The life-style a person is born into is normal for that child. For some, normal is living in the suburbs; attending bright, clean schools; and going to church on Sunday morning. For others, normal is a decaying ghetto, schools with bars on the windows, and drug pushers on the corner. The life-style learned in childhood dramatically affects all of life. It is this life-style that first tells us who we are and what the world is all about.

The Elementary Learner

Sunday school teachers do a much better job when they understand who they are teaching.

ELEMENTARY LEARNER NEEDS[6]

First, elementary children need love, acceptance, and security—the foundation on which everything else is built. Second, they need choices and challenges. They need to have some choice in what and how they learn and to be challenged by it. Elementary children are far too bright and curious to be bored for long.

Henrietta Mears is said to have remarked that it is a sin to bore children with the Bible. I think she was right. Allowing choice and creating a challenging, exciting learning experience will keep us from such a sin.

Third, the children in our Sunday school classes need praise and recognition. Their emerging self-identity and self-esteem must be nourished by those around them. Fourth, to a child's parents the Sunday school teacher should be his biggest cheerleader. Finally, elementary children need both independence and responsibility. They need the chance to try their wings. And, just as important, they need the chance to attempt and to fail in a safe, loving environment.

ELEMENTARY LEARNER CHARACTERISTICS[7]

Each stage of life has its own unique characteristics. That is certainly true of elementary children.

Physical Development

Elementary children are energetic. They are driven to do, to be active. Someone once said that Sunday school teachers tell their students to "sit still." However, at the same time, God leans over the balcony of heaven and whispers in their ears, "Wiggle! Wiggle!" Of course, the children always listen to God.

The elementary child's seemingly boundless energy may be frustrating for the teacher who wants his class to sit still and be quiet. This is unfortunate for a couple of reasons. First, whether adults like it or not that is the way children are. To expect children to sit quietly for an hour can make Sunday school a miserable environment for both teacher and child.

Second, the child's natural energy and curiosity create wonderful opportunities for exciting learning. The wise Sunday school teacher will seize those opportunities for the good of the child and the glory of God.

I am not suggesting that the Sunday school teacher should lose control of the class. I am suggesting that good classroom control is not defined by rows of quiet, motionless children. An active, exciting class is a much better and more "controlled" learning environment than a lecture hall.

One other physical characteristic should be noted. As with their younger brothers and sisters, elementary children develop at different rates. Children of the same age and in the same class may be very different. This is especially true of older elementary girls who may enter puberty months or years before other girls or their male classmates. Teachers need to be sensitive to these differences.

Emotional Development

Elementary students are a bundle of emotions. They are often insecure and uncertain. Their actions may be tentative and demonstrate a lack of self-confidence. The teacher should be especially sensitive to this need the first few weeks of the year and with newcomers. Everything possible should be done to help the child feel comfortable with the teacher and the other students.

Elementary children can be exasperating perfectionists.

Everything has to be just right. This tendency can lead to a great deal of frustration and discouragement. If things do not go well, some children may tend to quit. The teacher should be aware of this characteristic and offer his approval and encouragement. Such expressions will reassure the child and help him see the value in his efforts.

Another obvious and sometimes annoying characteristic of elementary children is their need for independence. In the classroom, this need of the students may collide with the teacher's legitimate need for control.

Finally, elementary children may be very impatient with their classmates, their teachers, and themselves. Perhaps the best way to teach patience is for the teacher to demonstrate patience.

Social Development

Several outstanding and often contradictory characteristics are obvious in the elementary child. First, he is outgoing and friendly. Given the opportunity, children will usually accept and become friends with a new child. This gregarious quality can be a great advantage to the Sunday school as it endeavors to reach unchurched children. At the same time, elementary children may also be painfully shy. The teacher needs to be aware that shyness can dominate a class and plan ways to encourage the children's natural friendliness.

Elementary children are group-conscious and concerned about having a "best friend." They need both the acceptance and security of the group and the intimacy of a best friend. The importance of the group and the child's loyalty to it may be seen in the emphasis on team play one observes on school playgrounds.

However, the need for group acceptance and for a best friend can work against each other. The Sunday school teacher needs to help each child feel part of the class and allow times when close friendships may develop.

Elementary children are also very competitive and concerned

with who is best. This characteristic represents both a great danger and a great opportunity. Teachers often use competitive activities in the Sunday school class. Competition is great for the child who wins. But it may be devastating for the child who loses. Competitive activities should be designed so that everybody wins. Many people have had their self-concept destroyed by childhood games. It should never happen in the Sunday school.

Intellectual Development

The elementary child's attention span is an important issue. The teacher should plan the lesson with his students' average attention span in mind. For example, for a second-grade class of 7-year-olds, no activity should last more than 7 minutes. If a longer and more complex creative learning activity is planned, it should be broken down into a series of activities, each of which lasts no more than 7 minutes.

The teacher must also be concerned with his students' intellectual development. Children simply do not develop emotionally, physically, or intellectually at the same rate. That can be clearly seen in the varying reading abilities found in any given class. The teacher should be close enough to his students to know each one's abilities and to plan accordingly. This fact argues for a variety of creative learning activities in the class. Many different activities allow participation by students with varying abilities.

Finally, the teacher needs to recognize that each student has an individual learning style. As with intellectual development, the teacher must take the various learning styles into account and plan accordingly. Again, the most practical way to address this need is to plan a variety of creative learning activities, allowing each student to find one that meets his needs.

CENTER STAGE

Childhood presents a great opportunity to build a strong foundation of biblical knowledge. Much of what a person needs to know about God, the Bible, the church, and the Christian life can and should be taught in childhood. That information provides the necessary foundation for future learning, developing positive relationships, and living a Christian life-style.

The characteristics and circumstances of the childhood learner point to an emphasis on information. Children are actively inquisitive and delight in discovery. The elementary child's natural competitiveness, perfectionism, and honest desire to please the Sunday school teacher create opportunities to teach biblical content.

Life-Style Education and the Elementary Child

While content is at center stage for the elementary child, it should be taught in a way that takes into account the emotional, relational, and behavioral impact.

KNOWLEDGE

Because elementary children have a short attention span the lesson should include several different kinds of activities. Beginning the session with activities that prepare the children for the lesson can set a positive tone for the day. The Bible story should be told in a clear and dramatic fashion. Creative learning projects should be part of each lesson.

In addition, several other items are important. First, children need an opportunity to talk about their lives and the lesson with their teacher and classmates. Second, if at all possible, music should be a part of the lesson. Finally, choices are important. A variety of creative learning activities from which the students may choose meets a number of student needs and helps the children get excited about learning. It also meets the children's need for independence.

EMOTIONS

The Sunday school teacher needs to consider four emotional factors. First, elementary children, like their younger brothers and sisters, need to feel secure. They also need to be protected from each other. Children are capable of saying and doing cruel things to each other.

Next, elementary children are perfectionists and easily frustrated. They require activities that are appropriate to their needs and abilities. The activities should be difficult enough to challenge but not so difficult as to frustrate.

Third, the children are seeking independence and need supportive and controlled freedom, such as choosing between several different learning activities.

Finally, elementary children need patience. They can be quite exasperating, but—like everyone else—they are still in the process of becoming.

ACTION

Creative learning activities should be carefully chosen. They should vary in type and take into account the different skills and abilities of the learners. The activities may take a number of forms, including games, music, drama, art, creative writing, and others. While each activity can be used and enjoyed by the class, the key is to have several different ones available so the children can have some choice in selecting one.

Beyond the use of creative Bible learning activities, older elementary children especially may take part in organized class ministry. The ministry may range from missions projects, such as Boys and Girls Missionary Crusade, to service projects, such as helping to clean an older person's house.

RELATIONSHIPS

Again, an appropriate student-teacher ratio is critical if the Sunday school teacher is to build a quality relationship with his students. One teacher per eight students is a good rule of thumb. It will give the teacher a chance to minister to each child and build a close relationship with him.

Equally important are the relationships the students develop with each other. The teacher should encourage the students to build positive relationships with each other as well as with the teacher. Emphasis should be placed on team building, cooperation, and loyalty to each other.

Students need to develop positive relationships with the teacher and with the other students. But they also need to develop a personal and positive relationship with God. The teacher should encourage this relationship by building in opportunities for the children to pray, worship, and praise as part of the Sunday school hour.

We do not know how individual members of a Sunday school class will turn out. But we do know Sunday school will have a profound impact. What kind of impact is up to us.

NOTES

[1]Anne Orland, *Children Are Wet Cement* (Old Tappan, N.J.: Fleming H. Revell Co., 1981).

[2]Donna Harrell and Wesley Haystead, *Creative Bible Learning for Young Children Birth–5 years* (Ventura, Calif.: Regal Books, 1977), 18–21.

[3]Keith Drury and Sharon Drury, *Children as Learners* (Winona Lake, Ind.: Light and Life Press, 1979), 23–34.

[4]James Michael Lee, *The Flow of Religious Instruction* (Birmingham, Ala.: Religious Education Press, 1973), 116–118.

[5]Lucie W. Barber, *The Religious Education of Preschool Children* (Birmingham, Ala.: Religious Educational Press, 1981).

[6]Barbara Bolton and Charles T. Smith, *Creative Bible Learning for Children Grades 1–6* (Glendale, Calif.: Regal Books, 1977), 31–37.

[7]Drury, *Children as Learners,* 52–77.

9

Life-Style Education for Youth and Adults

Perhaps the most famous Bible story about a teenager is of David and Goliath (1 Samuel 17). Rejecting Saul's armor, David faced the giant alone with only a sling, five smooth stones, the foolhardy courage of youth, and the presence of God.

They were enough. When Goliath moved to attack, David ran to meet him, hurled his stone, and struck the Philistine in the forehead. David's decision to fight Goliath set his life on a course that ultimately brought him to the throne of Israel.

The story of David and the giant provides an interesting analogy of what confronts modern youth. Like David, they face a seemingly impossible task. Their giant challenge is to successfully navigate the waters of youth and become adults. Like Saul, adults try to help. But all too often their solutions, like Saul's armor, do not fit. Like David, they are often misunderstood and criticized by their own family. Like David, each young person must face his giant alone with whatever resources he has at hand. And, more often then not, like David, young people conquer their giant and win the rewards of adulthood.

Choosing a Life-Style

The junior high, high school, and college years are a magical time of life. It is a time to see, "who we are and what we can be." It is a time for the person to establish his own distinct identity and discover his abilities, interests, and potential.

During this time, young people must make dozens of critical choices. Those choices determine, to a large extent, the rest of life. Young people must decide whether or not to go to college, whether or not to marry, and choose a vocation. Along with these big decisions, they must also make dozens of other critical choices that will dramatically affect all of life. Once made, many of these decisions can never be unmade. What one's life will be like tomorrow is largely determined by choices made today.

Youth, therefore, may best be thought of in terms of *choosing* a life-style. Preschool children catch their family's life-style, elementary children conform to that life-style, but young people actively choose a life-style. They may choose one very similar to their parents' and friends' or something entirely different.

The Teenage Learner

This time in life lasts for a decade; from age 12 to 22, from junior high through college. We will consider three distinct periods: junior high, senior high, and college.

JUNIOR HIGH[1]

Five outstanding characteristics mark the junior high years. First, the physical changes and rapid growth young people experience as they enter puberty make it an awkward and difficult period. Next, young people experience a heightened sense of self-awareness. They are obsessed with how they look, what they wear, who they are seen with, and doing what's "in."

Equally important is the strong social pressure the junior high student faces. This is the period of life when fitting into a group is the single most important issue in life. It is particularly important to be in the "in" group. Young people join groups to help them feel secure, to affirm their self-identity, and for self-defense. Junior high is a place where everyone dresses alike, talks alike, and acts alike to prove they are different.

Another important characteristic is the emotional sensitivity with which junior high students must deal. One of the side effects of puberty and the physical changes is this heightened sensitivity.

Finally, these young people are beginning the process of developing character. Until this point in life they have held and been held accountable to their parents' standards of right and wrong. Now, for the first time, they are hearing other voices. Parental authority declines as peer influence grows. They begin the arduous process of sorting out who they are as distinct from their parents and friends.

SENIOR HIGH[2]

Senior high, an equally critical period of life, is marked by some outstanding characteristics. First, the awkwardness of puberty has faded into physical maturity. This maturity is not troublesome on the football field or basketball court. But sexual maturity may be quite troublesome for the youth, his parents, and the Sunday school. Senior high students have acquired physical maturity but lack the emotional maturity needed to deal with sexual needs and desires.

Second, senior high students have an increased intellectual ability. The concrete thinking of junior high has matured into an awareness of the world around them and the ability to think abstractly.

Third, these students have developed a social conscience. It is not just a consciousness of society, but a conscience by consensus. They are dependent on their peer group for much of their sense of right and wrong. But their ability now encompasses much more than their younger brothers and sisters.

Finally, senior high is a time of spiritual openness in which young people search for answers to life's most difficult questions. As graduation day approaches, with all of its significance, there is increasing pressure to settle these issues. It is a time when faith is seriously considered and may be adopted or rejected.

COLLEGE

Not everyone in our society goes to college. But whether a young person enters college, the military, or the work force he must deal with several key issues in the first 5 years after high school.[3]

Who am I?

First, and most critical, is the issue of self-identity. An identity crisis can be a real part of this stage of life. For some it seems quite easy. For others, it is a very trying and confusing time of sorting, accepting, rejecting, and experimenting.

Next, this is a period of rebellious independence. Many college-age students mistakenly believe that to have an identity of their own they must rebel against the identity provided by their family and society. Linked to this desire for independence is a new relationship with authority. Once feared and followed, authority is now resented and resisted.[4]

How do I relate?

New relationships are another of the critical issues faced by college-age youth. They must develop new relationships with their parents and society as adults. Many people marry during these years. In addition, many become parents. They take on new roles and responsibilities and are expected to relate to others within those new roles. College-age people are in the process of forming sexual and identity roles. These roles of husband, wife, father, mother, lover, man, and woman shape and define much of life.

What should I believe?

This age-group solidifies the beliefs, attitudes, and values that shape their adult life. That involves dealing with the values they learned as children from their parents and church, the values of their peers, and those of society. Often what emerges is a blend of all three. Whether for good or bad, these are the values they own, that establish their unique identity and govern their relationships and behavior.

OVERARCHING ISSUES

While junior high, senior high, and college students have unique needs, all three groups share some characteristics. First, other youth are vitally important to them. Second, they feel tremendous pressure to fit in, to be part of the group. Third, most young people bow to the pressure and conform. Fourth, in one way or another, all young people are trying to come to grips with their independence and work out their relationships with authority, including their parents, the church, and the school. Finally, all young people are concerned with the here and now.

Although these issues and characteristics may create an explosive mix, they also create unequaled opportunity.

CENTER STAGE

At center stage for junior high, senior high, and college-age youth are relationships. It is true that the content, emotional impact, and behavioral outcomes of the Sunday school are as critical at this age as at any other. However, the wise youth teacher will spotlight relationships. Building healthy relationships with peers, parents, authority figures, and the opposite sex are the major challenge and top priority.

The Sunday school teacher should first endeavor to build a positive relationship with his students. There are several wrong ways to go about it. One is to try to imitate the students. Acting like the students does not build a good relationship, it just provides some comic relief. Some teachers think that abdicating their authority is the only way to build a positive relationship with their students. It is not. Anarchy in the classroom destroys relationships.

Building a strong teacher-student relationship requires several key ingredients. First, the teacher must genuinely love his students. Young people are drawn to people who really care about them. Next, the teacher must be genuine and transparent. Kids can spot a hypocrite miles away. The teacher must also treat his students with the respect due a brother or sister in Christ. No one likes feeling inferior. Being approachable, open, and trustworthy are other important qualities. Finally, the teacher must be the teacher, the authority in the class.

Building a positive teacher-student relationship is only part of the task. The Sunday school teacher must provide the opportunity and security necessary for the students to build positive relationships with their peers. Young people need opportunities to talk to each other. Helping new and shy students make friends and feel accepted is an important part of being a good Sunday school teacher. Finally, the Sunday school class should do things together outside the classroom.

A young person's relationship to authority figures is a third critical area. His natural drive for independence and a sense of self-identity often brings him into conflict with adult authority at home, work, church, and school. The Sunday school teacher can help his students develop a positive relationship to authority by modeling biblical authority. Biblical authority is loving, fair, patient, and predictable. Biblical authority is about love and service, not power and control. It is more concerned with what is good for the student than for the teacher. That kind of authority builds positive relationships.

Last, and perhaps most important, are positive parent-child relationships. Young people often find themselves at odds with their parents. Sunday school teachers should never compete with a parent for a student's affections. Nor should they ever interfere with the parent's legitimate rights and responsibilities. On the other hand, Sunday school teachers can befriend both parent and child. They should help parents and children better understand each other. Finally, the Sunday school can provide opportunities for parents and their children to minister and have fun together.

Life-Style Education and Youth

Applying life-style education principles to young people is extremely important.

KNOWLEDGE

The biblical content and the way that content is studied are equally important. Particular attention should be given to helping the young people make the connection between their lives and the Scriptures. Their here-and-now orientation makes relevance a real concern. This need for relevance extends to the selection of subjects for study.

Learning should build on, not repeat, what has been learned before. A junior high class may study the same biblical material as their younger brothers and sisters, but it should not be studied in the same way. Students need to be guided to discover the underlying principles and spiritual truths of a Bible story.

Biblical content should be presented in a way that invites maximum participation from the learners. Discussion groups, music, creative art, writing projects, and question-and-answer periods are all ways to provide firsthand discovery of God's Word.

Especially important are learning activities that capitalize on the relational priority of youth. Peer pressure is real, but it does not have to be bad. Peer pressure can encourage people to do what is right, as well as what is wrong. It can be an ally of the Sunday school and the gospel.

EMOTIONS

The teacher should be especially aware of the young person's self-conscious sensitivity and create a warm, accepting, and safe environment. He should never belittle or allow others to belittle or embarrass his class members. On the contrary, the teacher should go out of his way to affirm each learner. He should not tolerate cruel words or actions by anyone in the class.

The teacher should also be sensitive to the emotional volatility of this age-group. These years can be very stormy, and the storms may sweep into a Sunday school classroom. To deal successfully with emotional upheaval, the teacher needs to be sensitive and understanding, and help the student to put the crisis in perspective, develop patience, and roll with the waves. Overreacting makes the situation worse, not better.

ACTION

Young people are active learners, and they learn more when they are actively involved. An active class reduces discipline problems and is more likely to build positive student-teacher and student-student relationships.

When used in conjunction with creative Bible-learning activities, the lecture is a powerful tool. However, when used alone week after week its effectiveness diminishes dramatically. This is true for several reasons.

First, the lecture goes against the grain of many young people because it is contrary to their need for independence. Second, it has a very low relational value. Finally, many youth reject what adults say simply because adults say it. The lecture has its place, but it must be used wisely.

The teacher should help his students make the connection between what the Bible teaches and the student's daily life. It is too easy for the young person to compartmentalize his learning and see no connection between what he learned on Sunday and how he lives.

Finally, the Sunday school class is an ideal launching pad for ministry and active participation in the life of the church. The students can do service projects that benefit people in the church or community. They can engage in short-term home and foreign missions ventures. They can initiate and lead Bible clubs and other witnessing activities in their schools and neighborhood. Providing such opportunities is a logical and necessary part of the Sunday school's ministry to youth.

RELATIONSHIPS

We have already spent a good deal of time discussing the importance of relationships in the life-style education of young people. What needs to be added here is an emphasis on the relational quality inside and outside of the classroom. If the

Sunday school teacher hopes to have an effective ministry, he must build strong relationships with his learners. Without them nothing else will succeed.

David defeated his giant. So will most of the young people in our Sunday schools. They will become adults with or without our help, and perhaps in spite of it. But that is not enough. David went on to fulfill God's call in his life. In doing so, he had the help of Samuel, his family, his friends, and God. If young people are to grow to adulthood and be like Jesus, they too must have our help.

> When I was a child, I talked like a child, I thought like a child, I reasoned like a child. When I became a man, I put childish ways behind me (1 Corinthians 13:11).

Carrying Out a Life-Style

Malcolm Knowles identifies five assumptions about the ways children and adult learners are different. Children are assumed to be dependent learners, while adults are self-directed. Teachers can assume that adults bring a rich resource of experience to the learning event that children do not. A child's readiness to learn is based on his age-level, but adult readiness develops from life's tasks and problems. Adult learners are task- and problem-oriented, not subject-centered. Finally, adults are motivated to learn by internal incentives and curiosity, while children are motivated by external rewards and punishment.[5]

The Adult Learner

Who is an adult? That is not always an easy question to answer. When the legal voting age was 21 and the draft age was 18, many young people thought that if they were adult enough to serve in the military, they should be old enough to vote. We have all met people who were chronologically adults but emotionally or intellectually children.

RECOGNIZING AN ADULT[6]

For our purposes, we will consider someone an adult who has

aged beyond the typical college years. By that time most people have settled into an adult life-style. While having reached a certain age does not mean one has reached a certain level of maturity, it is handy to think of adulthood as beginning at a certain point. But there are and always will be exceptions to that rule.

Adults demonstrate interest and attitude stability. Gone are the days of meteoric changes and the instability of immaturity. Another characteristic of adulthood is settling on an occupation. The person no longer asks himself what he would like to be when he grows up, but starts wondering, *Is that all there is?*

Finally, adults fulfill roles in society. Spouse, employee, citizen, and parent are only a few of the roles an adult is expected to play.

In his ground-breaking research, Levinson divides adult life into three periods: early adulthood, ages 22–40; middle adulthood, ages 45–60; and late adulthood, age 65 and older. These periods are separated from each other by transition stages. Within each period are various stages and transitions. This approach led one person to comment that adults are going into, are in, or are just coming out of a crisis all of their lives.[7]

YOUNG ADULTS

During the young-adult years, the person is consumed with a number of extremely important tasks. He is in the process of selecting a mate and adapting to a married life-style. Most young adults are busy starting a family and raising young children. They are learning to manage their own households and are actively engaged in building their careers and finding a social group.

MIDDLE ADULTS

Middle adults face a different agenda. They are absorbed with civic and social responsibilities. Establishing and maintaining economic stability is a high priority. Their children are now teens, and they are concerned with guiding their children to adulthood. As their children grow and leave home, the parents are faced with the empty-nest syndrome and the need to establish a new and different kind of relationship with each other. They now have more leisure time and must adjust to the physical changes of age.

Finally, while still parenting their own children, many middle adults must care for their aging parents. This is the "sandwich" generation during which adults shoulder tremendous economic and emotional burdens.

OLDER ADULTS

Growing old presents its own agenda. These adults must deal with the physical changes of old age, as well as the economic and emotional realities of retirement. The death of friends and family members is a harsh reality, and it brings a stark realization of the older adult's own mortality. Older adults also are involved in social and civic activities, but the emphasis shifts. Finally, they are forced to adjust to being old in a society where youth is the most valued age.

ADULT LEARNERS

Despite their differences, all adult learners share some common characteristics. First, adults do not have a learner's attitude. They have their own definite ideas and personal experience, which contribute to a sense of independence. Next, adult learners desire immediate application of what they learn. Their participation in learning events is voluntary, and they are often apprehensive about learning situations. They learn best through their own efforts, identify readily with groups, and want feedback.

As learners, adults are interested in their needs.[8] That fact creates important opportunities for the Sunday school. What adults feel they need to know is what they are interested in, what they want to know. The gospel meets the adult learner at that level with the answers to life's needs and predicaments.

CENTER STAGE

At center stage for adult learners is living out their chosen life-style. What adults know, how they feel, and the quality of their relationships are all critically important. However, in adulthood people have the greatest opportunity to put their knowledge, feelings, and insights into practice. James said it this way,

> Do not merely listen to the word, and so deceive yourselves. Do what it says. Anyone who listens to the word but does not do what it says is like a man who looks at his face in a mirror and, after looking at himself, goes away and immediately forgets what he looks like (James 1:22–24).

Living out a Christian life-style is the crucial emphasis for a number of reasons. First, it is consistent with the needs, interests, and concerns of adult learners. It is where they are in their lives. Adulthood is the time in life when the understanding, attitudes, and relationships developed over a lifetime are expressed in a life-style. The nature of adult life mandates an emphasis on behavioral goals in the Sunday school.

Power is a second reason to focus on action in the adult Sunday school classroom. In any church, as in society at large, adults are in control. If they act consistently with what they believe, they can dramatically influence the church, their families, their work, and the community, and help build the Kingdom. If they do not, disaster may result.

Adults are also the role models and shapers of the next generation. The influence of parents, Sunday school teachers, and other adult leaders cannot be overemphasized. By living consistently adults provide positive models for others. Inconsistency discredits the faith and creates a false impression of what it means to be a Christian. The future of the church is impacted by both.

Finally, a concern for consistent Christian living mirrors scriptural concern. Paul called the Corinthians "mere infants" because there was "jealousy and quarreling" among them (1 Corinthians 3:1–3). God's will is that each Christian "grow up into him" so the body of Christ can build itself up "as each part does its work" (Ephesians 4:15,16).

Life-Style Education and the Adult Learner

While the adult Sunday school class should focus on behavioral goals, it must not neglect the other areas.

KNOWLEDGE

Material presented in the classroom must be applicable to adult learners, chosen with their needs and interests in mind. In doing so, it is important not to avoid issues that may seem boring or too controversial if they are vital to Christian living. If the believer stays only with what is safe or interesting, vital areas of Christian growth and development will be overlooked and spiritual growth will be stunted.

Helping adults develop Christian maturity means teaching all the Bible, not just the parts they are interested in. The key is a balanced presentation of all the Bible has to say on a subject and then helping adults see why it is important and how it applies to their lives.

Adults want and need to be active participants in their own learning. Methods that involve adults in the discovery of biblical principles and insights into their application should be employed. Discussion, games, simulations, group projects, art, music, creative writing, and other techniques can greatly enhance the adult Sunday school's impact.

EMOTIONS

Adults, like any other learners, need to feel accepted by the group. They need to feel valued and respected by their peers and their teacher.

Adults come to Sunday school with very real needs. They need to feel that people in the class care about them and what they are going through. Adults want to know and be known. They need to feel that they belong and are important to others.

Those needs are best met in the class that encourages face-to-face, student-to-student interaction. Using small groups and other involvement methods helps the students feel they are important and valued members of the class.

Finally, adults are more capable than younger learners of dealing with their beliefs, attitudes, and values. Confronting cherished beliefs with the gospel's claims may be an uncomfortable process for the teacher and learners. However, it is an important part of the Sunday school's ministry.

ACTION

Adults need opportunities to apply and express what they learn in the classroom through ministry and service. Mobilizing the adult class to action is as much a part of the Sunday school teacher's responsibility as preparing the Bible study.

Ministry and service activities are important for a number of reasons. First, they reinforce what is learned in the classroom. Second, they provide valuable insights into the Christian life and spiritual maturity. Finally, such projects demonstrate the practicality of the claims of Christ to those doing and those receiving the ministry.

But there are also things the teacher can do. First, each class session should challenge the learners to consider ways to apply what they have learned. Identifying ways to carry out the lesson should be followed by trying to secure a commitment from the learners that they will indeed act on the lesson.

Second, the teacher can encourage class members to talk about how they applied previous lessons. Such "testimonies" reinforce the learning, encourage others to act, and help the teacher determine his effectiveness.

Finally, the teacher can encourage the learners to form accountability groups within the class. In groups of two or three, class members agree to pray for each other, support each other, and hold each other accountable for how they applied the lesson. In this way, class members "spur one another on toward love and good deeds" (Hebrews 10:24).

RELATIONSHIPS

The adult Sunday school class makes building relationships possible by presenting learning activities that encourage people to interact, by providing opportunities for social interaction in and out of the class, and by encouraging people to do ministry and service together.

Lecture as the sole teaching method works against developing good relationships by preventing interaction. On the other hand, creative learning activities in which the learners work in pairs, triads, or small groups create opportunities for people to make friends. Get-acquainted activities before or after class help people find out about each other and can make a valuable contribution.

Peter Pan never wanted to grow up. Some Christians are like that. Their bodies grow older, but they never mature spiritually. The adult Sunday school should help believers "reach unity in the faith and in the knowledge of the Son of God and become mature, attaining to the whole measure of the fullness of Christ" (Ephesians 4:13).

NOTES

[1]Roy G. Irving and Roy B. Zuck, *Youth and the Church* (Chicago: Moody Press, 1968), 97–103.

[2]Ibid., 111–116.

[3]Ibid., 128.

[4]Lawrence O. Richards, *You and Youth* (Chicago: Moody Press, 1973), 42–47.

[5]Malcolm S. Knowles, *The Modern Practice of Adult Education* (New York: Cambridge, The Adult Education Company, 1980), 390.

[6]Monroe Marlowe and Bobbie Reed, *Creative Bible Learning for Adults* (Ventura, Calif.: Regal Books, 1977), 24–25.

[7]Daniel J. Levinson, *The Seasons of a Man's Life* (New York: Ballantine Books, 1978), 57.

[8]Earl F. Zeigler, *Christian Education of Adults* (Philadelphia: The Westminster Press, 1960), 42–45.

10

Tripod: The Sunday School, the Spirit, and the Saints

Some people think Sunday school is an outdated way to help people come to Christian maturity. They are looking for new and better ways. Some churches have replaced Sunday school with other functions, and others have simply stopped having it. They believe they have found a better way or that Sunday school is no longer workable. Eventually they find out they were wrong.

Is Sunday school the old way? Yes. Have new ways been developed? Yes, by the dozens. Has a better way been found? I do not think so.

The traditional Sunday school has many advantages over other approaches. First, it already exists in most churches. It does not have to be created. Second, Sunday school has a proven track record. Over the years we have learned how to make Sunday school effective. We are a long way past the trial and error process that any new approach must go through. Third, Sunday school has proven its effectiveness. Generations of Christians attest to the fact that Sunday school is a highly effective way to help people become like Jesus.

Finally, Sunday school is a natural for life-style education. Built into the Sunday school are the organizational structure, small-group atmosphere, age-grading, and other features essential to life-style education. No other single program offers that combination.

Sunday school has fallen into disfavor in some circles for a number of reasons. Some churches have succumbed to the lure of the new. They reason that new is better than old. Others have experienced Sunday schools that were not very good. That negative experience made them look for something better. Still others fail to see the need for any form of Christian education because they view the church as a worshiping not a studying community. Finally, for some pastors Sunday school is a tiresome program that does not seem to do much for the church.

I am not suggesting that Sunday schools are always good. They are not. Nor would I suggest that they do not take a tremendous amount of energy and resources. They do. Nor would I suggest that they have the same sparkle and excitement of something new. They do not. Finally, I am not suggesting that the church should not be a worshiping community. It should.

What I am saying is that the Sunday school has all the necessary ingredients for successful Christian education. Sunday schools have always provided a strong biblical-content base. Millions of dollars and man-hours have been spent to develop high-quality Bible-study material. The Sunday school class has the capacity for being an exciting, emotionally satisfying place. It is also a place where beliefs, attitudes, and values can be taught and tried. It is a perfect launching pad for Christian service and ministry. Finally, the Sunday school by its nature is a relational environment.

The problem with our Sunday schools, then, is not the concept. It is that we do not carry out the concept very well. The football coach may call the perfect play, but if the team does not execute it well the quarterback will get sacked. Sunday school is a good game plan. But pastors, teachers, and administrators also have to do a good job.

Strategies for Successful Sunday Schools

Sunday school can do the job. But if our Sunday schools are to be successful, they must address some crucial issues.

FOCUS ON VALUES

First, the Sunday school must go beyond teaching Bible facts and address the issues of core values and principles for living. Biblical information must be included and available, but the information must reach beyond that level to a consideration of the Bible's meaning to the individual and his life. The teacher should not assume the learners share common beliefs. He should be willing to assist the individual in his exploration of the Bible and his examination and evaluation of his beliefs and behavior.

If the educational experience is based on information only, or if there is no opportunity for interaction, there is little hope of significant impact. If, on the other hand, the learners are encouraged to interact with the issues and determine their significance in their lives, they will be much more likely to gain from that experience.

FOCUS ON RELATIONSHIPS

Second, Sunday school must be a place where learning occurs in a highly relational environment. A supportive, caring environment in which learners feel free to express their insights and relate their experiences will enhance the Sunday school's positive impact. It is through such interactions that people are stimulated to reconsider their life-styles as they come in contact with others who share their experiences.

Such relationships can have a powerful impact long after the educational experience is past. The teacher should remember that other people stimulate the awareness of inconsistencies and are also the primary resource for resolving such inconsistencies.

FOCUS ON AWARENESS

Third, the Sunday school should be a place where people become more aware of what the Bible teaches and of how they are living. Research indicates there are three ways people become aware that they are not living up to what they believe: through other people, confrontation, and experience.[1]

The Sunday school class is a place where learners can be confronted with the gospel's claims, come in contact with other

Christians, and experience ministry and the life of Christ. The wise Sunday school teacher will utilize these resources.

Educational methods that encourage people to talk to each other, meaningful classroom and nonclassroom experiences, and confrontation with the claims of Christ are crucial.

Finally, the Sunday school teacher should give his learners the opportunity to reflect on what they have learned and its meaning in their lives. They need the chance to think through an issue and express their feelings and insights. Knowing what the Bible means and applying that understanding to life is far more valuable than just knowing what it says.

FOCUS ON DISCOVERY

Fourth, the Sunday school should be a place where students can explore what the Bible says and how it applies to their lives. The teacher's willingness to allow and encourage the learners to seek out and pursue issues that are meaningful to them is essential. Also critical is an awareness of the resources and resource people that can help in that exploration. The Sunday school class should be just the launching pad for a week-long examination of what the Bible teaches. Exploring new ways to live is an important part of becoming more like Jesus.

FOCUS ON NEEDS

Fifth, the Sunday school must be individual- and life-oriented and willing to meet needs. A Sunday school teacher who is available to his learners and willing to meet their needs is vital. An educational experience is much more likely to help people become like Jesus if it meets them at their point of need and encourages them to take responsibility for their own spiritual development. Without that kind of personal stake in the learning process it is unlikely the learner will deal with life's issues at the core-values level.

FOCUS ON MATURITY

Sixth, pastors, Sunday school administrators, and teachers must recognize that modeling the Sunday school on the information-based, public school system does not advance the cause of Christian maturity. It may actually impede the Christian's growth and development. The Sunday school's goal is not to provide information, but to help people become like Jesus.

FOCUS ON QUALITY

Seventh, we have to get serious about Sunday school. Its ministry has been degraded, trivialized, and demeaned. Changing this trend must begin where it started—in the pulpit. Pastors must once again recognize that the church's mission is to disciple believers and that the Sunday school is their single most effective ally.

Laymen must also take their Sunday school ministries seriously and invest the time, effort, and energy required for effective ministry. Good Sunday schools do not just happen. They take plenty of hard work. If lay teachers and administrators do not value the Sunday school and recognize what it can be, it is doomed to failure. Teaching people to obey the gospel is fulfilling the Great Commission.

FOCUS ON CHOICE AND RESPONSIBILITY

Eighth, the Sunday school must again emphasize that people are responsible for the choices they make. While there are many things about our lives we cannot choose, we are free to make real choices within the circumstances of life. Not only must we choose to follow Christ as Savior, but we must also daily choose to make Him our Lord.

FOCUS ON EXPERIENCE

Ninth, the Sunday school must point its learners to a personal experience and a personal relationship with Jesus Christ. Fundamentally, Sunday school ought to be a profoundly spiritual experience. By its very nature, Sunday school is the process of bringing learners into contact with the living Word of God. Sunday schools do not fail because of a lack of interest, or of teachers, or of enthusiasm. Sunday schools lack interest, teachers, and enthusiasm because they fail spiritually.

FOCUS ON SPIRITUAL LIFE

Finally, pastors, teachers, and administrators must return to a dependence on the Holy Spirit. Training, facilities, supplies, and equipment are all important ingredients in the successful Sunday school. But they are meaningless without the power and presence of God's Spirit. Only a Spirit-powered Sunday school can do the job.

The Scriptures repeatedly warn us that human wisdom is really folly. "There is a way that seems right to a man, but in the end it leads to death" (Proverbs 14:12). We are encouraged to "trust in the Lord with all [our] heart and lean not on [our] own understanding" (Proverbs 3:5). We need to remind ourselves of what God said in Isaiah 55:8,9.

> "My thoughts are not your thoughts, neither are your ways my ways . . . . As the heavens are higher than the earth, so are my ways higher than your ways and my thoughts than your thoughts."

The secret to a truly successful Sunday school is total dependence on God.

The Conclusion of the Matter

Some people would argue that to be like Jesus is an impossible goal. Christians have been, are, and always will be inconsistent. That is true. And when that fact reflects a stagnant spiritual life it is tragic. But in another sense it is not sad at all. Growing Christians will always be inconsistent. Whenever they reach a certain level of Christian living they discover there is another level. And they begin again. They "press on toward the goal to win the prize for which God has called" us (Philippians 3:14). In that process they become more and more like Jesus.

> *To be like Jesus,*
> *To be like Jesus,*
> *All I ask,*
> *To be like Him;*
> *All thru life's journey,*
> *From earth to glory,*
> *All I ask,*
> *To be like Him.*[2]

To be like Jesus is the only truly worthy goal of the Christian life. Just think about it. What would the church and our world be like if every Christian were conformed to the image of Jesus Christ? Just think of what could be if we were all like Him. . . .

NOTES

[1]Burkhart, "Discrepancies Between Belief and Behavior," 166–169.
[2]*Melody Choruses,* 3.

Bibliography

Ajzen, Icek, and Martin Fishbein. "Attitude–Behavior Relations: A Theoretical Analysis and Review of Empirical Research." *Psychological Bulletin* 84, no. 5 (1977): 888–918.

Allport, G. W. "Religion and Prejudice." *Crane Review* 2 (1959): 1–10.

Barber, Lucie W. *The Religious Education of Preschool Children.* Birmingham, Ala.: Religious Educational Press, 1981.

Blasi, Augusto. "Bridging Moral Cognition and Moral Action: A Critical Review of the Literature." *Psychological Bulletin* 88, no. 1 (1980): 1–45.

Bolton, Barbara, and Charles T. Smith. *Creative Bible Learning for Children Grades 1–6.* Glendale, Calif.: Regal Books, 1977.

Borgida, Eugene, and Bruce Campbell. "Belief Relevance and Attitude–Behavior Consistency: The Moderating Role of Personal Experience." *Journal of Personality and Social Psychology* 42, no. 2 (1982): 239–247.

Burkhart, Robin. "Discrepancies Between Belief and Behavior: Implications for Adult Education." Ann Arbor, Mich.: University Microfilms International, 1987.

Cacioppo, J.T., S.G. Harkins, and R. Petty. "The Nature of Attitudes and Cognitive Responses and Their Relationship to Behavior." In *Cognitive Responses in Persuasion,* ed. Richard Petty, Thomas Ostrom, and Timothy Brock. Hillsdale, N.J.: Lawrence Erlbaum Associates, Pub. Co., 1981.

Cappella, J., and J. Folger. "An Information Processing Explanation of Attitude–Behavior Inconsistency." In *Message–Attitude–Behavior Relationship: Theory, Methodology and Application,* ed. Donald Cushman and Robert McPhee. New York: Academic Press, 1980.

Davidson, Andrew R., and James J. Jaccard. "Variables That Moderate the Attitude–Behavior Relation: Results of a Longitudinal

Survey." *Journal of Personality and Social Psychology* 37, no. 8 (1979): 1364–1376.

Davidson, Andrew R., Steven Yantis, Marel Norwood, and Daniel E. Montano, "Amount of Information About the Attitude–Object and Attitude–Behavior Consistency." *Journal of Personality and Social Psychology* 49 (1985): no. 5, 1184–1198.

Drury, Keith, and Sharon Drury. *Children as Learners.* Winona Lake, Ind.: Light and Life Press, 1979.

Dykstra, Craig R. *Vision and Character: A Christian Educator's Alternative to Kohlberg.* New York: Paulist Press, 1981.

Gauthier, David P. "Moral Action and Moral Education." In *Moral Education: Interdisciplinary Approaches,* ed. C.M. Beck, B.S. Crittenden, and E.V. Sullivan. New York: Newman Press, 1971.

Gross, Steven Jay, and C. Michael Niman. "Attitude–Behavior Consistency: A Review." *Public Opinion Quarterly* 39, no. 3 (1975): 358–368.

Harrell, Donna, and Wesley Haystead. *Creative Bible Learning for Young Children Birth–5 years.* Ventura, Calif.: Regal Books, 1977.

Hogan, Robert. "Moral Conduct and Moral Character: A Psychological Perspective." *Psychological Bulletin* 79, no. 4 (1973) 217–232.

Insko, C. A., and J. Schopler, "Triadic Consistency: A Statement of Affective–Cognitive–Conative Consistency." *Psychological Review* 74 (1967): no. 5, 361–376.

Irving, Roy G., and Roy B. Zuck, *Youth and the Church.* Chicago: Moody Press, 1968.

Israel, A. "Some Thoughts on Correspondence Between Saying and Doing." *Journal of Applied Behavior Analysis* 11, no. 2 (1978): 271–276.

Joy, Donald M., ed. *Moral Development Foundations: Judeo–Christian Alternatives to Piaget/Kohlberg.* Nashville: Abingdon Press, 1983.

Karlan, G., and F. Rusch. "Correspondence Between Saying and Doing: Some Thoughts on Defining Correspondence and Future Directions for Application." *Journal of Applied Behavior Analysis* 15, no. 1 (1982): 151–162.

Kelman, Herbert C. "Attitudes Are Alive and Well and Gainfully Employed in the Sphere of Action." *American Psychologist* 29 (1974): 324.

Knowles, Malcolm S. *The Modern Practice of Adult Education.* New York: Cambridge, The Adult Education Company, 1980.

Krebs, D., and A. Rosenwald. "Moral Reasoning and Moral Behavior in Conventional Adults." *Merrill-Palmer Quarterly* 23, no. 2 (1977): 77–87.

LaPiere, Richard T. "Attitudes vs. Actions." In *Attitude Theory and*

Measurement, ed. Martin Fishbein, 26–31. New York: John Wiley & Sons, Inc., 1967.

Lee, James Michael. *The Flow of Religious Instruction.* Birmingham, Ala.: Religious Education Press, 1973.

—————. *The Shape of Religious Instruction.* Mishawaka, Ind.: Religious Education Press, 1971.

Levinson, Daniel J. *The Seasons of a Man's Life.* New York: Ballantine Books, 1978.

Leypoldt, Martha M. *Learning Is Change: Adult Education in the Church.* Valley Forge, Pa.: Judson Press, 1971.

Likona, Thomas, ed. *Moral Development and Behavior: Theory, Research and Social Issues.* New York: Holt, Rinehart and Winston Pub. Co., 1976.

Marcel, G. *The Mystery of Being, Part II.* Chicago: Henry Regnery Press Co., 1960.

Marlowe, Monroe, and Bobbie Reed. *Creative Bible Learning for Adults.* Ventura, Calif.: Regal Books, 1977.

McNamee, S. "Moral Behavior, Moral Development and Motivation." *Journal of Moral Education* 7, no. 1 (October 1977): 27–31.

McNaughton, A. "Can Moral Behavior Be Taught Through Cognitive Means?—Yes." *Social Education* 41, no. 4 (April 1977): 328, 331–332.

Melden, A.I. "Moral Education and Moral Action." In *Moral Education: Interdisciplinary Approaches,* ed. C. M. Beck, B. S. Crittenden, and E. V. Sullivan. New York: Newman Press, 1971.

Orland, Anne. *Children Are Wet Cement.* Old Tappan, N.J.: Fleming H. Revell Co., 1981.

Poole, M. S., and J. E. Hunter. "Behavior and Hierarchies of Attitudes: A Deterministic Model." In *Message–Attitude–Behavior Relationship: Theory, Methodology and Application,* ed. Donald Cushman and Robert McPhee. New York: Academic Press, 1980.

Regan, D.T., and R. Fazio, "On the Consistency Between Attitudes and Behavior: Look to the Method of Attitude Formation." *Journal of Experimental Social Psychology* 13 (1977): 28–45.

Richards, Lawrence O. *Creative Bible Teaching.* Chicago: Moody Press, 1970.

—————. *You and Youth.* Chicago: Moody Press, 1973.

—————. *A Theology of Christian Education.* Grand Rapids, Mich.: Zondervan Publishing, 1975.

Rokeach, M., and P. Kleijunas. "Behavior as a Function of Attitude–Toward–Object and Attitude–Toward–Situation." *Journal of Personality and Social Psychology* 22 (1972): 194–201.

Rokeach, Milton. *Beliefs, Attitudes and Values: A Theory of Organization and Change.* San Francisco: Jossey-Bass Inc., 1972.

—————. "Long-Range Experimental Modification of Values, Attitudes and Behavior." *American Psychologist* 26 (May 1971): 453–459.

Santrock, J. "Moral Structure: The Interrelations of Moral Behavior, Moral Judgment, and Moral Affect." *Journal of Genetic Psychology* 127 (1975): 201–213.

Wallen, N. "Can Moral Behavior Be Taught Through Cognitive Means—NO." *Social Education* 41, no. 4 (April 1977) 329–331.

Ward, Ted. *Values Begin at Home.* Wheaton, Ill: Victor Books, 1979.

Wicker, Allan W. "Attitudes vs. Actions: The Relationship of Verbal and Overt Behavioral Responses of Attitude Objects." *Journal of Social Issues* 25, no. 4 (1969b) 41–78.

————. "An Examination of the 'Other Variables' Explanation of Attitude–Behavior Inconsistency." *Journal of Personality and Social Psychology* 19, no. 1 (1971): 18–30.

Zeigler, Earl F. *Christian Education of Adults.* Philadelphia: The Westminster Press, 1960.